Level 2 · Part 1

Integrated Chinese

中文听说读写
中文聽說讀寫

CHARACTER WORKBOOK
Simplified and Traditional Characters

Third Edition

THIRD EDITION BY

Yuehua Liu and Tao-chung Yao
Yaohua Shi, Nyan-Ping Bi, Liangyan Ge

CHENG & TSUI COMPANY
Boston

22 21 20 19 18 17   7 8 9 10 11 12

Published by
Cheng & Tsui Company, Inc.
25 West Street
Boston, MA 02111-1213 USA
Fax (617) 426-3669
www.cheng-tsui.com
"Bringing Asia to the World"™

ISBN 978-0-88727-685-9

Cover Design: studioradia.com

Cover Photographs: Man with map © Getty Images; Shanghai skyline © David Pedre/iStockphoto; Building with masks © Wu Jie; Night market © Andrew Buko. Used by permission.

Interior Design: hiSoft

The *Integrated Chinese* series includes books, workbooks, character workbooks, audio products, multimedia products, teacher's resources, and more. Visit www.cheng-tsui.com for more information on the other components of *Integrated Chinese*.

Printed in the United States of America

CONTENTS

Preface

This completely revised and redesigned Character Workbook is meant to accompany the third edition of *Integrated Chinese Level II (IC II)*. It has been over ten years since the *IC* series came into existence in 1997. During these years, amid all the historical changes that took place in China and the rest of the world, the demand for Chinese language teaching/ learning materials has grown dramatically. We are greatly encouraged by the fact that *IC* not only has been a widely used textbook at the college level all over the United States and beyond, but also has become increasingly popular for advanced language students in high schools. Based on user feedback, we have made numerous changes so that the Character Workbook can become an even more useful tool for students of Chinese.

Stressing the importance of learning a new character by its components

Learning a new character becomes much easier if the student can identify its components. If a new character contains a component already familiar to the student, the stroke order of that component will not be introduced again. However, we will show the stroke order of all new components as they appear when we introduce new characters. When the student learns a new character, he or she can easily tell if a component in the character has appeared in previous lessons. If the stroke order for that component is not displayed, it means that the component is not new. The student should try to recall where he or she has seen it before. By doing so, the student can connect new characters with old ones and build up a character bank. We believe that learning by association will help the student memorize characters better.

Main features of the new Character Workbook

a. Both traditional and simplified characters are introduced in equal size
If a character appears in both traditional and simplified forms, we show both to accommodate different learner needs.

b. Pinyin and English definition are clearly noted
We have moved the pinyin and the English definition above each character for easy recognition and review.

c. Radicals are highlighted
The radical of each character is highlighted. Knowing what radical group a character belongs to is essential when looking up that character in a traditional dictionary where the characters are arranged according to their radicals. To a certain extent, radicals can also help the student decipher the meaning of a character. For example, characters containing the radical 貝/贝 (bèi, shell), such as 貴/贵 (guì, expensive), and 貨/货 (huò, merchandise), are often associated with money or value. The student can group the characters sharing the same radical together and learn them by association.

d. Stroke order is prominently displayed
Another feature that we think is important is the numbering of each stroke in the order of its appearance. Each number is marked at the beginning of that particular stroke. We firmly believe that it is essential to write a character in the correct stroke order, and to know where each stroke begins and ends. To display the stroke order more prominently, we have moved the step-by-step character writing demonstration next to the main characters.

e. A "training wheel" is provided
We also provide grids with fine shaded lines inside to help the student better envision and balance their characters when practicing.

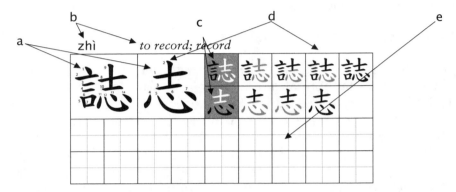

Other features in the new edition

A set of Chinese Character Crosswords have been added to each lesson. Students are asked to fill out the crossword puzzles based on the pinyin given, which helps them retain and re-associate characters when forming words.

To help the student look up characters more easily, we decided to provide two indices, one arranged alphabetically by pinyin and the other by lesson. The formation and radical of each character in this book are based on the fifth edition of the *Modern Chinese Dictionary* (現代漢語詞典第五版/现代汉语词典第五版) published by the Commercial Press (商務印書館/商务印书馆). A total of 201 radicals and the stroke number and stroke order of each character all appear in that dictionary, and in some cases the same character is listed under more than one radical. For the characters in this book that fall in that category, we provide two radicals in order to facilitate students' dictionary searches. The two radicals are presented in order from top to bottom (e.g., 名: 夕, 口), left to right (e.g., 功：工, 力), and large to small (e.g., 章: 音, 立; 麻: 麻, 广).

The changes that we made in the new version reflect the collective wishes of the users. We would like to take this opportunity to thank those who gave us feedback on how to improve the Character Workbook. We would like to acknowledge in particular Professor Hu Shuangbao of Beijing University, who read the entire manuscript and offered invaluable comments and suggestions for revision. Ms. Laurel Damashek at Cheng & Tsui assisted throughout the production process.

We hope you find this new edition useful. We welcome your comments and feedback. Please report any typos or other errors to **editor@cheng-tsui.com**.

Integrated Chinese

liàng *(measure word for vehicles)*

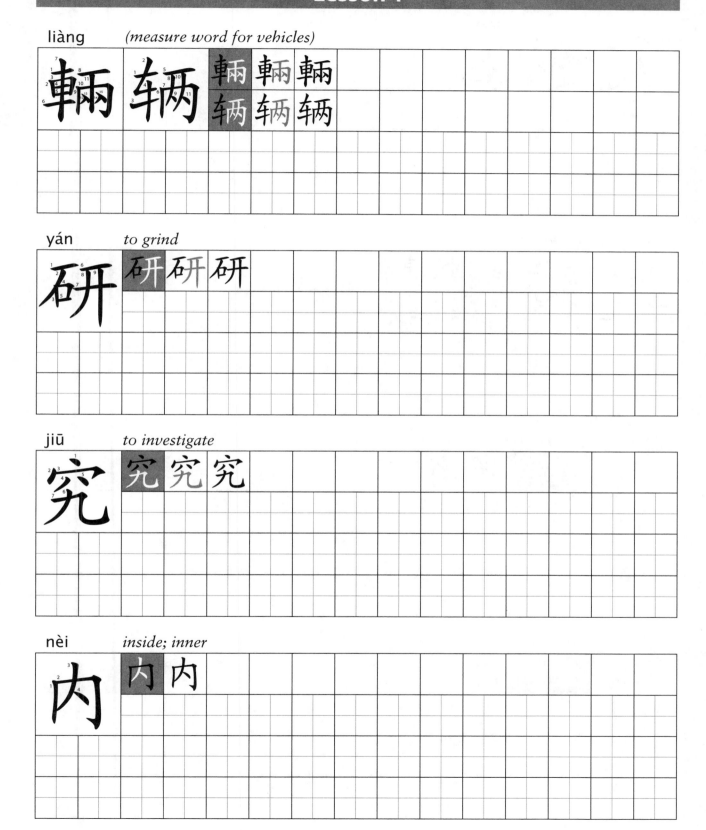

yán *to grind*

jiū *to investigate*

nèi *inside; inner*

quán   *complete*

全 全 全 全

jiào   *to compare*

較 較 較 較 較
較 較 較

shěng   *to save; to economize*

省 省 省 省 省

yóu   *from; out of*

由 由 由 由

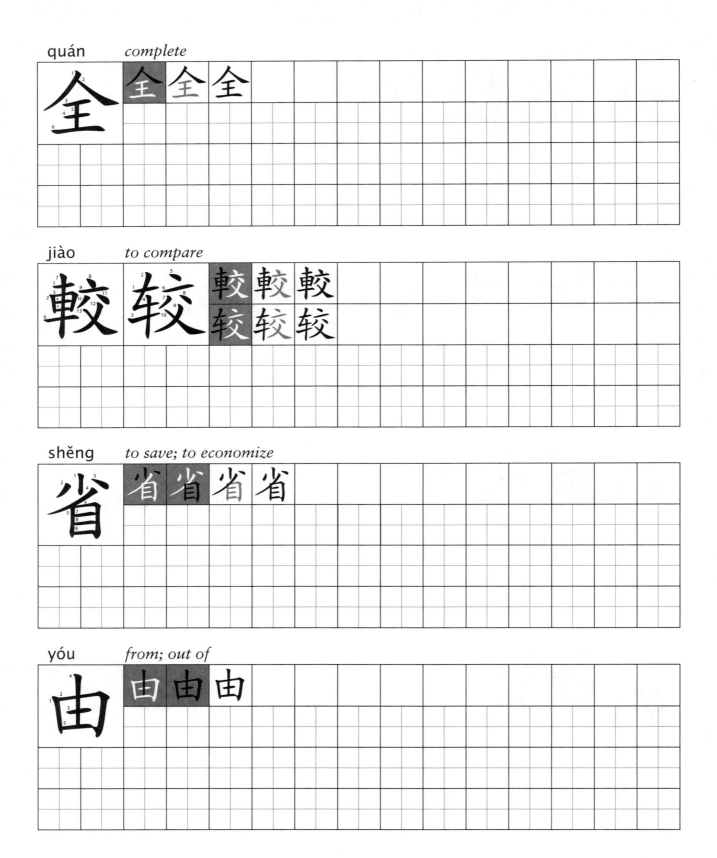

chù   *place*

處　处　處處處處處處處處
　　　處处处处

là   *to leave (something) behind*

拉　拉拉拉

Character from Proper Nouns

kē   *(a surname); handle of an axe; stem*

柯　柯柯柯

Chinese Character Crosswords

Fill out the puzzles based on the *pinyin* clues provided. The common character is positioned in the center of the cluster of rings. The arrows indicate which way you should read the words.

1.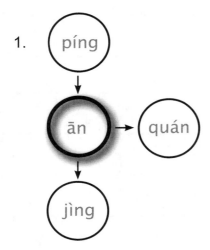

2.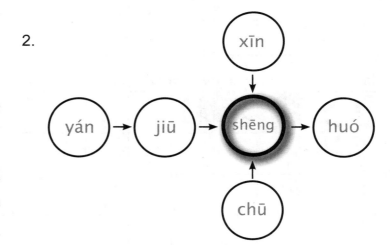

3.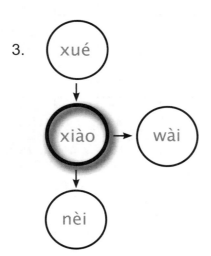

Lesson 2

wū   *room; house*

屋   屋 屋 屋

bǎi   *to put; to place*

擺 擺   擺 擺 擺 擺

tǎn   *blanket*

毯   毯 毯 毯 毯

guì   *cupboard; cabinet*

櫃 柜   櫃 櫃 櫃 櫃 櫃 / 柜 柜 柜 柜 柜 柜

guà   *to hang; to hang up*

掛 挂 掛 掛 掛 掛 掛
挂 挂 挂 挂

tiáo   *to regulate*

調 调 調 調 調
调 调 调

dòng   *(measure word for buildings)*

棟 栋 棟 棟 棟
栋 栋 栋

jiù   *(of things) old*

舊 旧 舊 舊 舊 舊 舊 舊 舊 舊
旧 旧 旧 旧

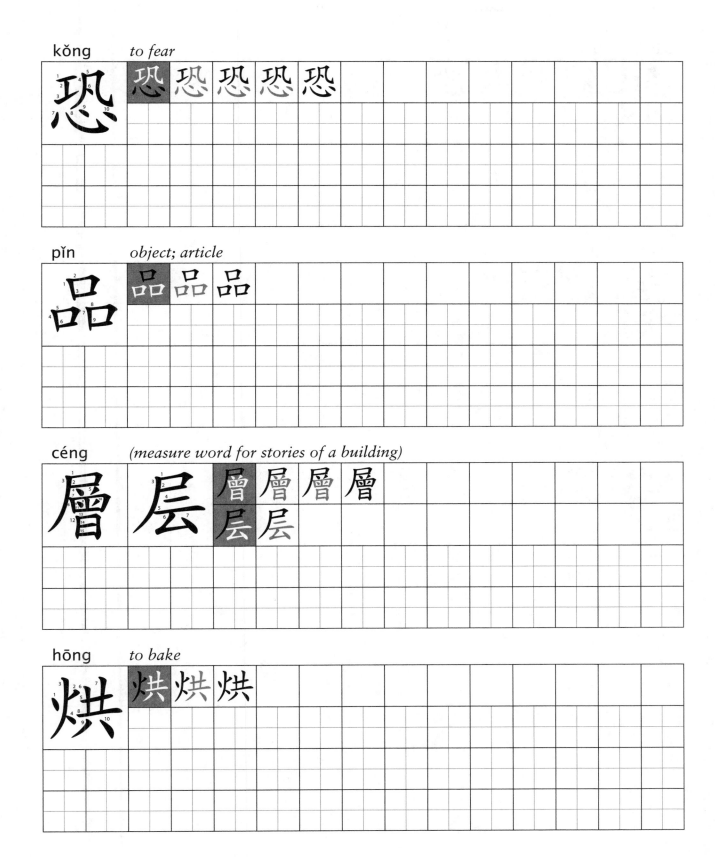

kǒng   *to fear*

恐

pǐn   *object; article*

品

céng   *(measure word for stories of a building)*

層 层

hōng   *to bake*

烘

bān   *kind; variety*

般 般 般 般 般

zháo   *to burn; to touch*

着 着 着 着 着

jí   *urgent*

急 急 急 急 急 急

Chinese Character Crosswords

Fill out the puzzles based on the *pinyin* clues provided. The common character is positioned in the center of the cluster of rings. The arrows indicate which way you should read the words.

1.

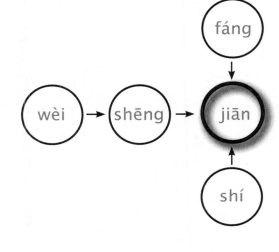

2.

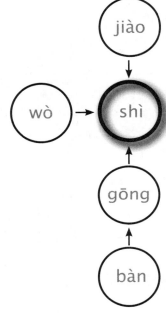

3.

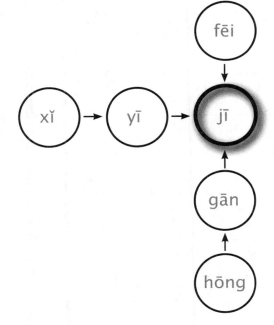

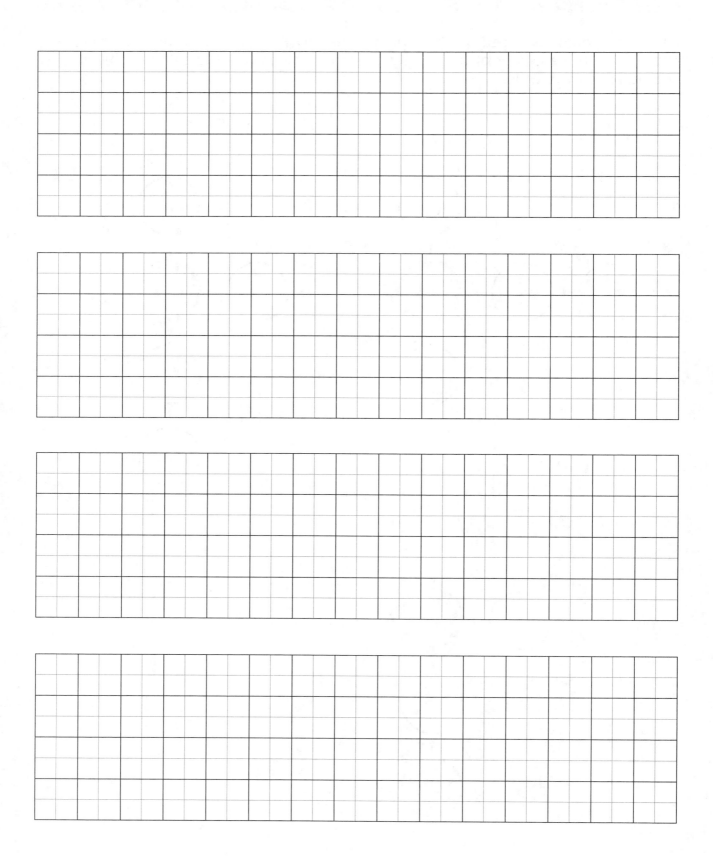

Integrated Chinese

Lesson 3

liú   *to leave behind*

留 留 留 留 留 留 留

jī   *chicken*

雞 鸡 雞 雞 雞 雞 雞 雞 雞 雞
鸡 鸡 鸡 鸡 鸡 鸡 鸡 鸡

zhēng   *to steam*

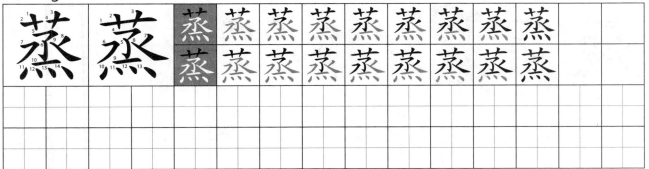

蒸 蒸 蒸 蒸 蒸 蒸 蒸 蒸 蒸
蒸 蒸 蒸 蒸 蒸 蒸 蒸 蒸 蒸

jiè   *mustard greens*

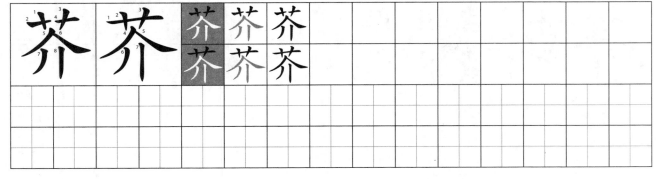

芥 芥 芥 芥
芥 芥 芥 芥

lán   *orchid*

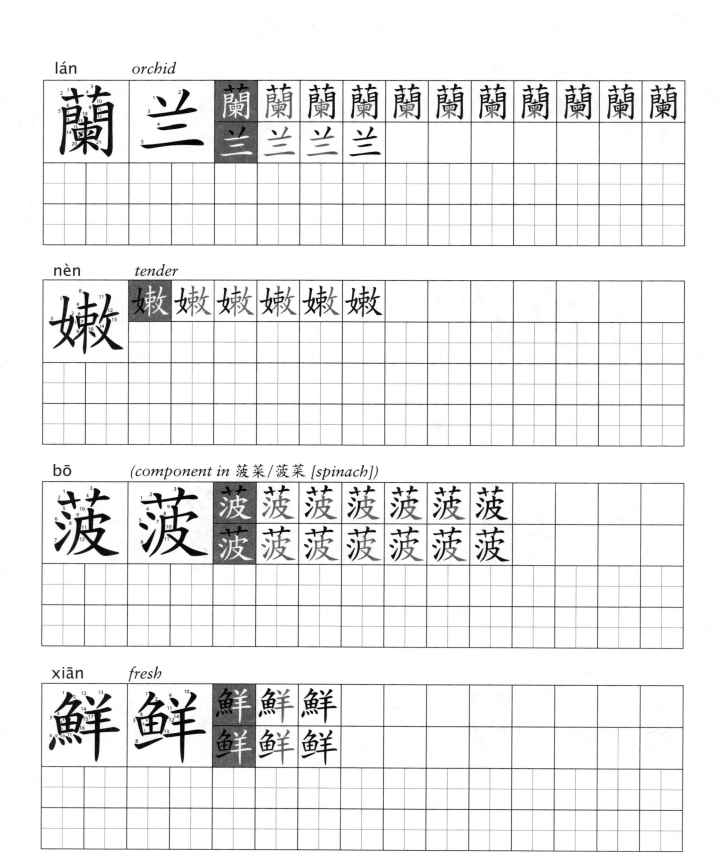

nèn   *tender*

bō   *(component in 菠菜/菠菜 [spinach])*

xiān   *fresh*

dàn *light in flavor or color*

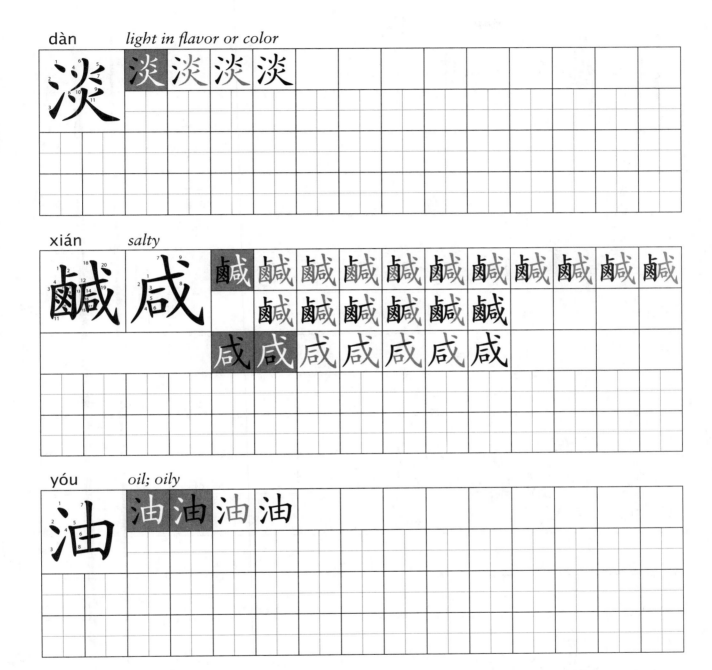

xián *salty*

yóu *oil; oily*

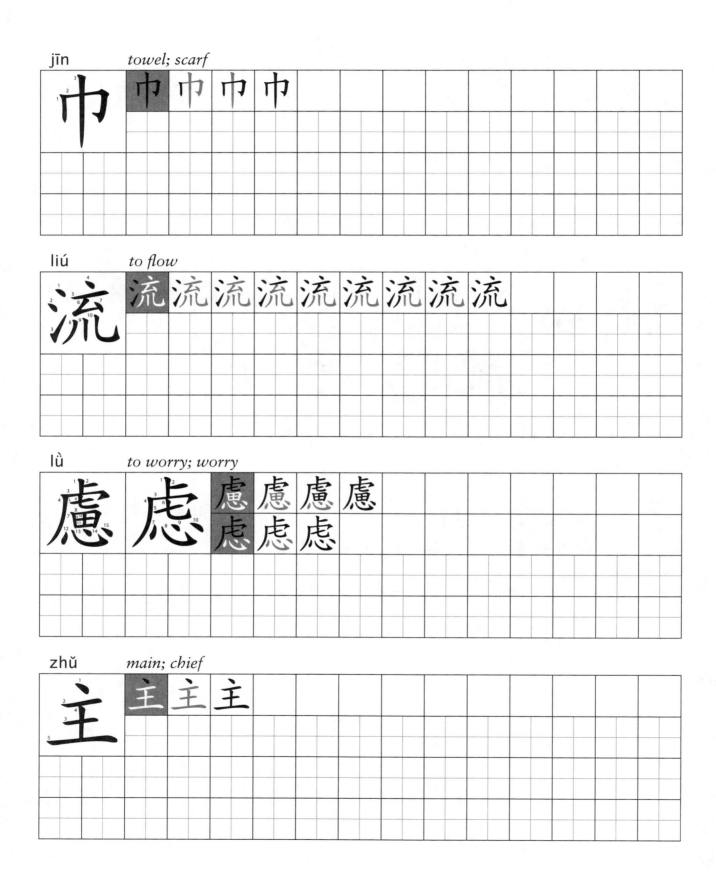

jīn　　towel; scarf

巾

liú　　to flow

流

lǜ　　to worry; worry

慮　慮

zhǔ　　main; chief

主

Characters from Proper Nouns

lì   *beautiful*

麗 丽 | 麗 麗 麗 麗 麗 麗 麗 麗 麗 麗 麗
麗 麗 麗 麗
丽 丽 丽 丽 丽 丽

shā   *sedge grass*

莎 莎 | 莎 莎 莎 莎
莎 莎 莎 莎

méi   *plum*

梅 | 梅 梅 梅

chuān   *river*

川　川 川 川 川

hú   *lake*

湖　湖 湖 湖 湖

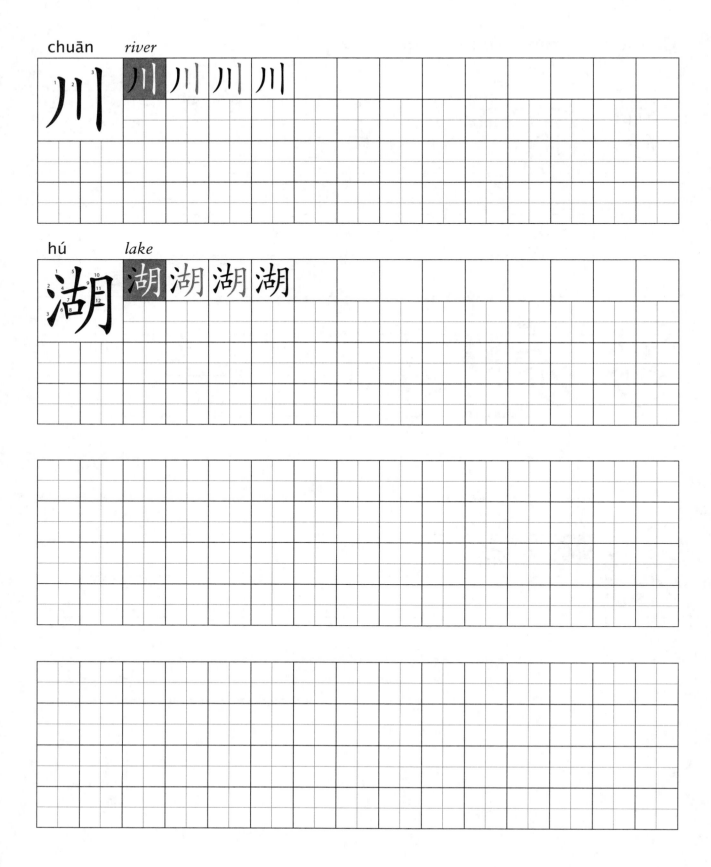

Chinese Character Crosswords

Fill out the puzzles based on the *pinyin* clues provided. The common character is positioned in the center of the cluster of rings. The arrows indicate which way you should read the words.

1.

zhī → dào ← wèi, dì →

2.

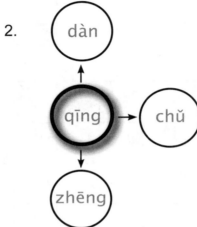

3.

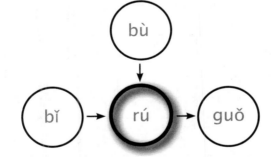

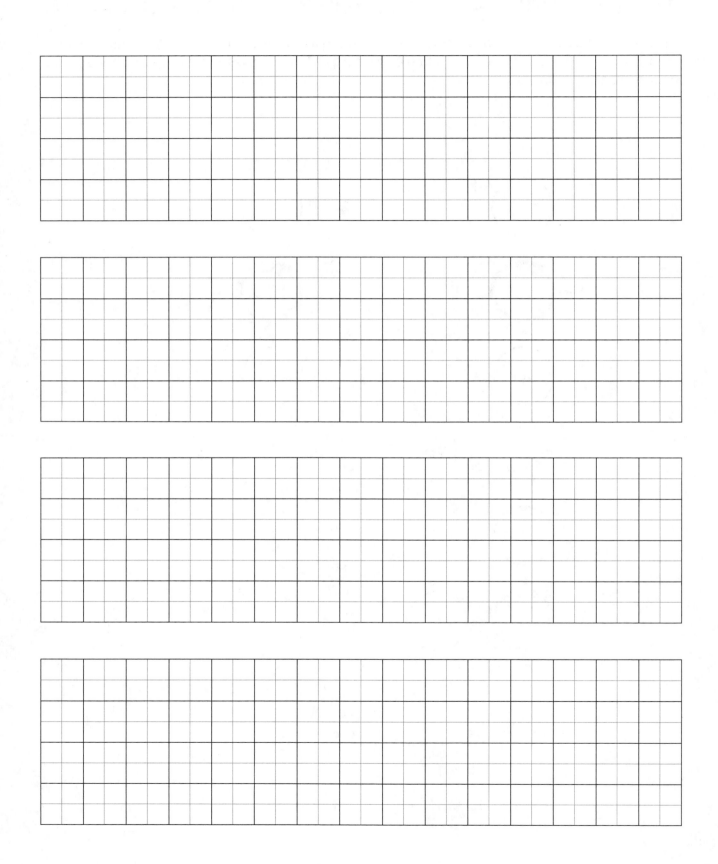

Integrated Chinese

Lesson 4

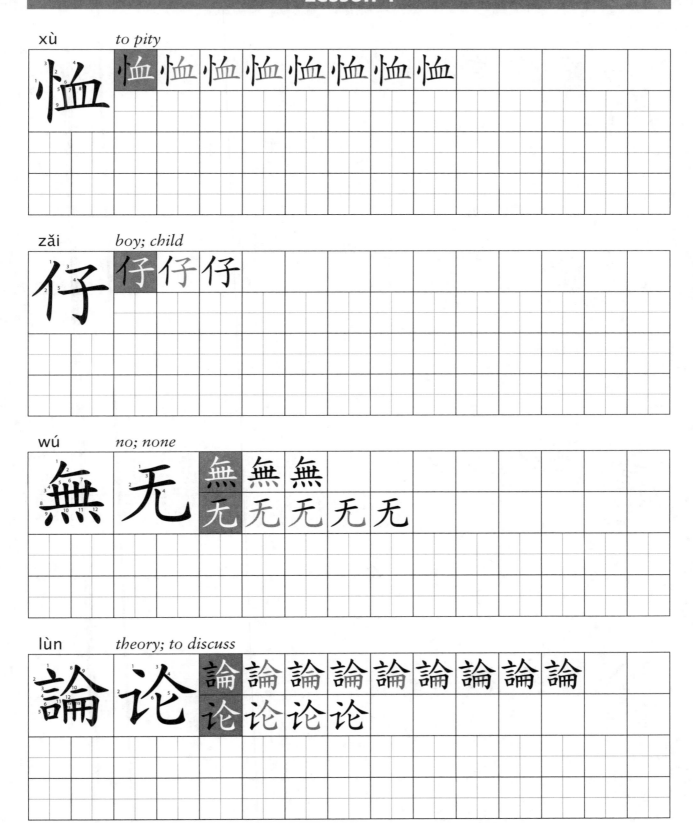

xù   *to pity*

恤

zǎi   *boy; child*

仔

wú   *no; none*

無 无

lùn   *theory; to discuss*

論 论

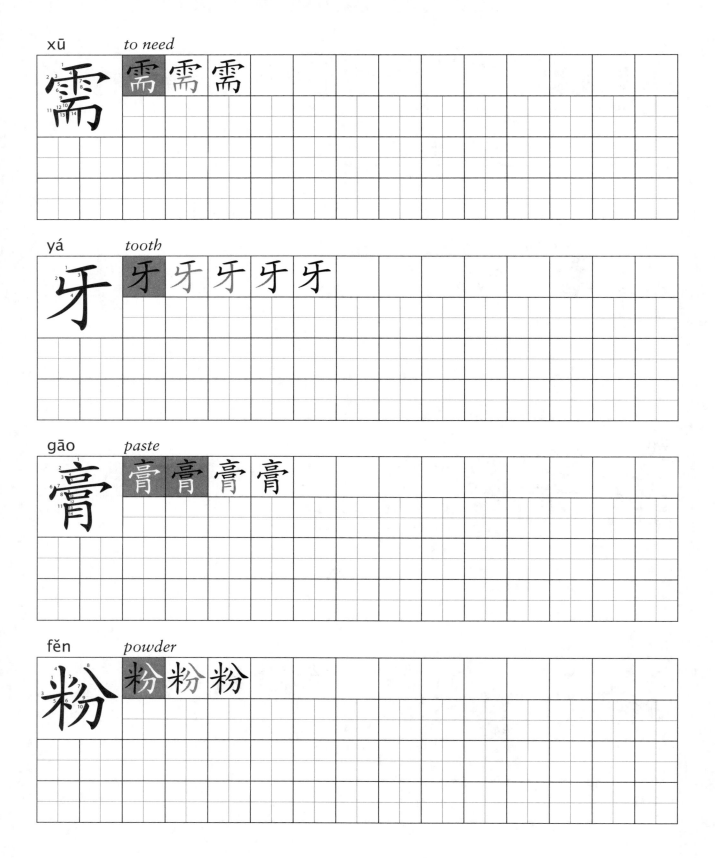

xū   *to need*
需

yá   *tooth*
牙

gāo   *paste*
膏

fěn   *powder*
粉

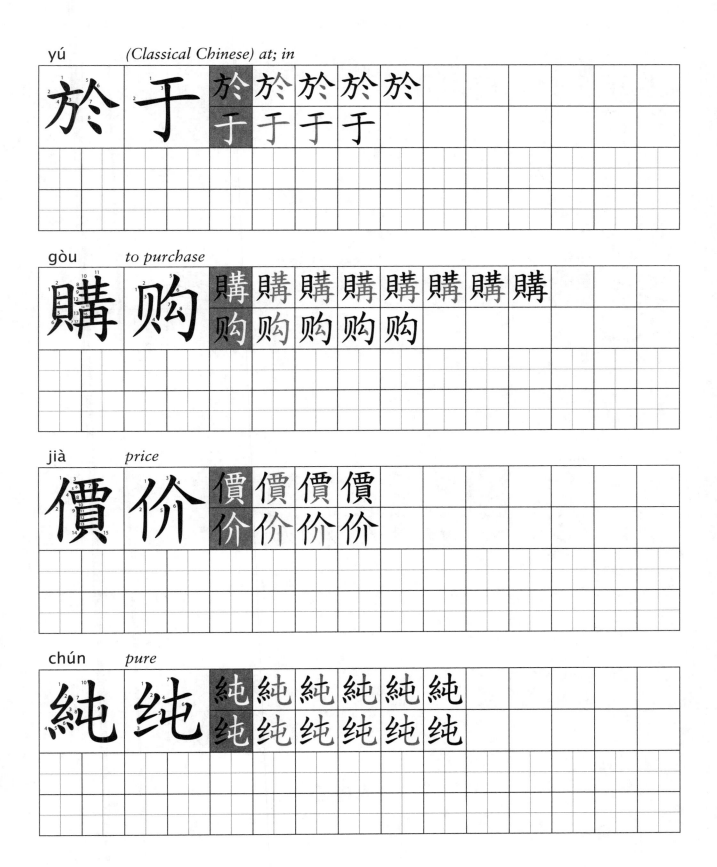

yú   *(Classical Chinese) at; in*

於 于   於 於 於 於 於
       于 于 于 于

gòu   *to purchase*

購 购   購 購 購 購 購 購 購 購
       购 购 购 购 购

jià   *price*

價 价   價 價 價 價
       价 价 价 价

chún   *pure*

純 纯   純 純 純 純 純 純
       纯 纯 纯 纯 纯 纯

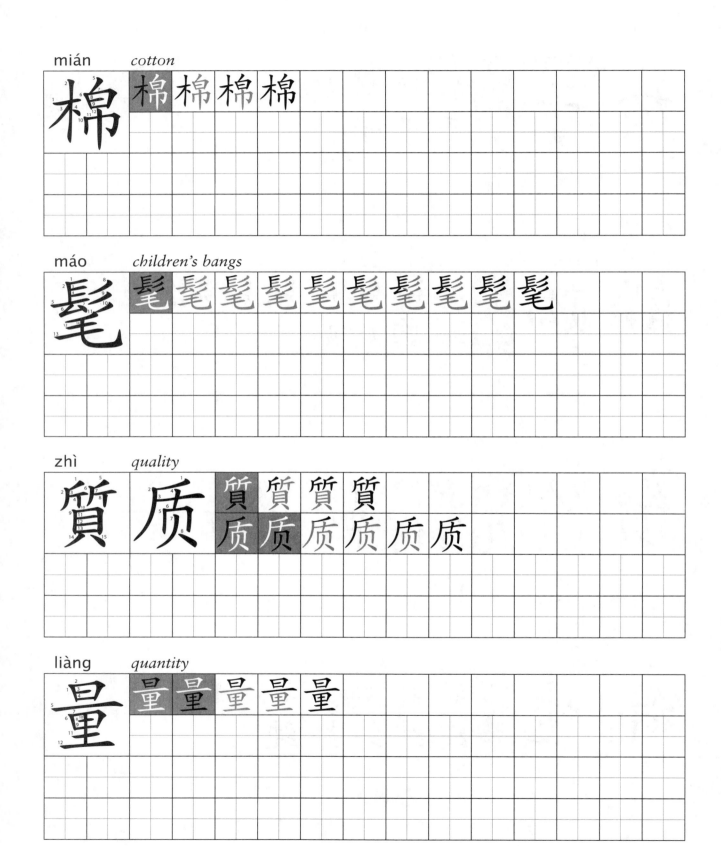

mián　*cotton*

棉　棉棉棉棉

máo　*children's bangs*

髦　髦髦髦髦髦髦髦髦髦髦

zhì　*quality*

質 质　質 質 質 質 / 质 质 质 质 质 质

liàng　*quantity*

量　量量量量量

bì   *must*

必   必 必 必 必 必 必 必

biāo   *mark*

標 标   標 標 標 標
          标 标 标

lián   *cheap; inexpensive*

廉   廉 廉 廉 廉 廉 廉 廉 廉 廉 廉 廉

hū,hu   *(Classical Chinese) in; at*

乎   乎 乎 乎 乎 乎 乎

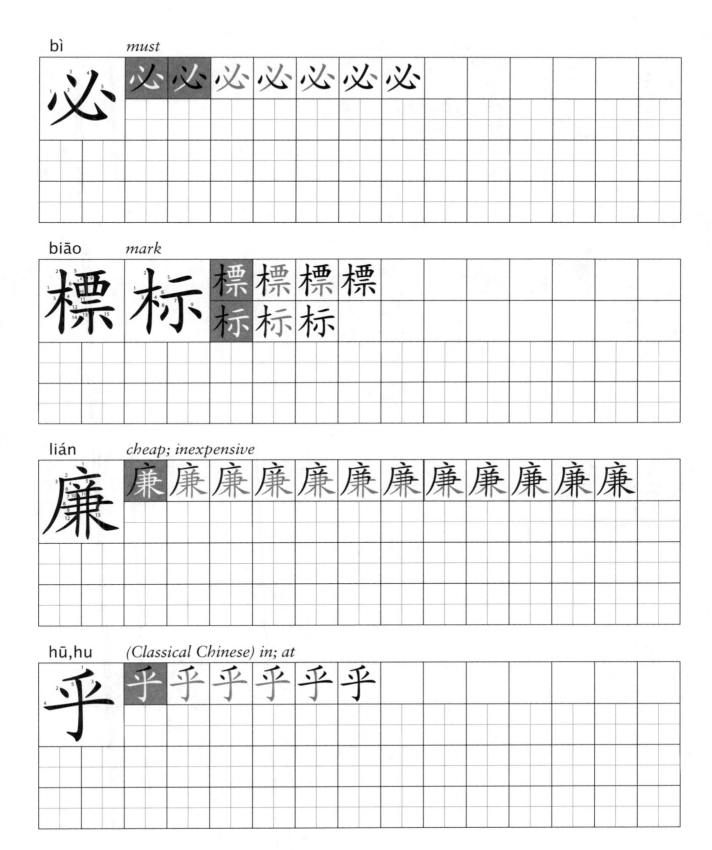

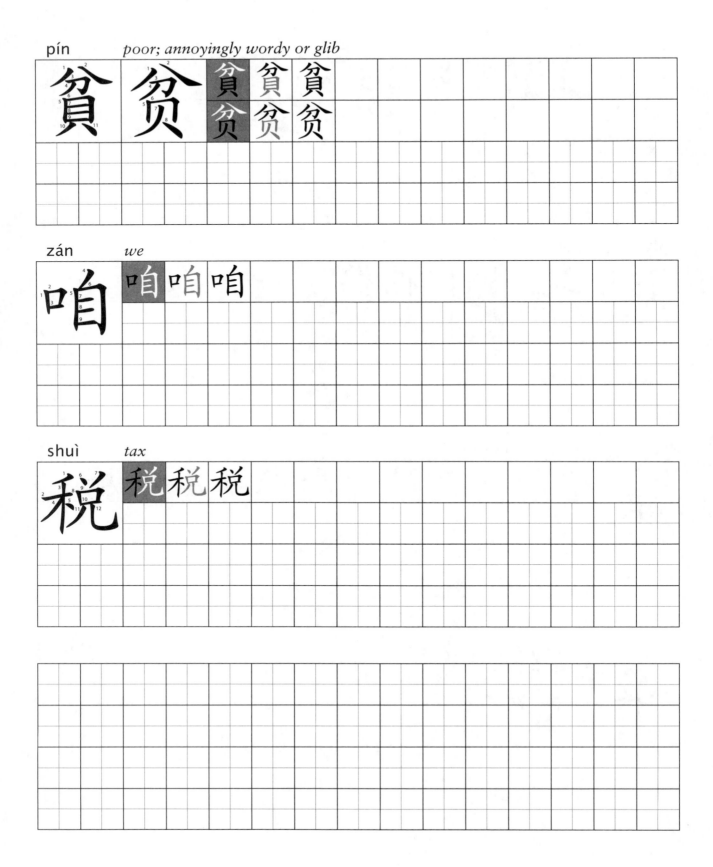

pín   *poor; annoyingly wordy or glib*

zán   *we*

shuì   *tax*

Chinese Character Crosswords

Fill out the puzzles based on the *pinyin* clues provided. The common character is positioned in the center of the cluster of rings. The arrows indicate which way you should read the words.

1.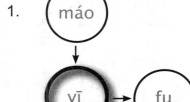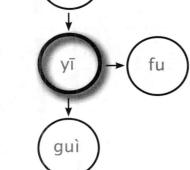

2.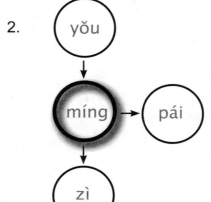

3.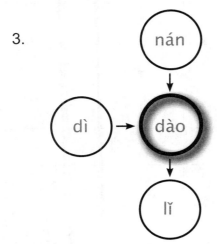

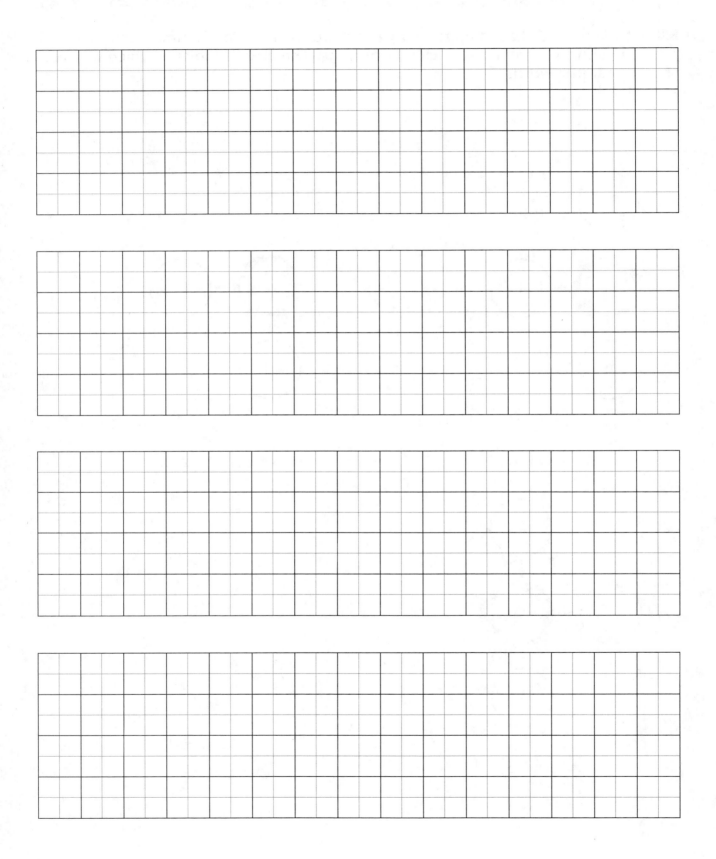

Integrated Chinese

xuǎn   *to choose*

選 选

shì   *world*

世

jiè   *realm*

界

lì   *to experience; experience*

歷 历

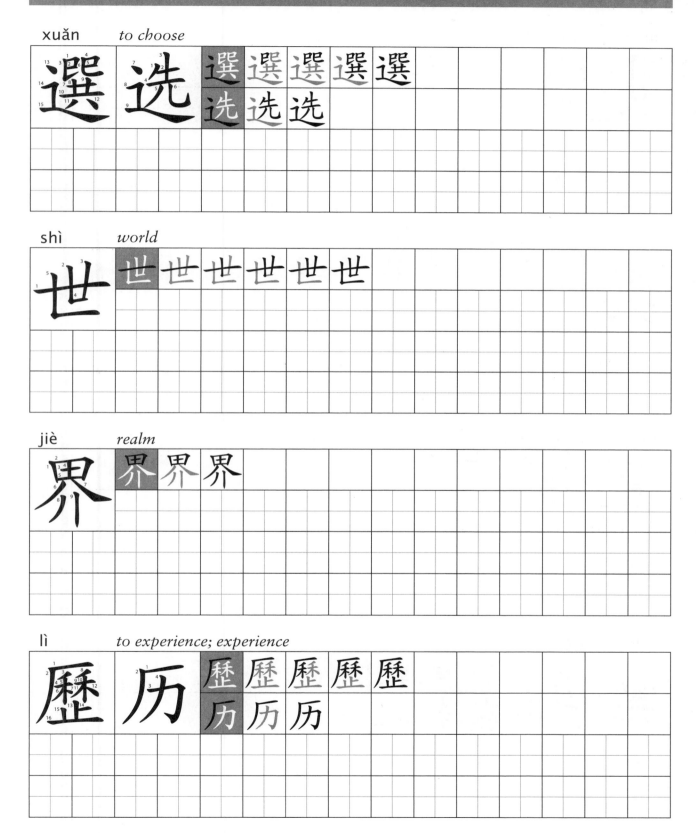

shǐ   *history*

史   史 史 史 史

qí   *(Classical Chinese, third person possessive pronoun)*

其   其 其 其 其 其 其 其 其

zhāng   *essay; article*

章   章 章 章 章

qīng   *light*

輕 轻   輕 輕 輕
          轻 轻 轻

sōng   *loose; relaxed*

鬆 松 鬆 鬆 鬆 鬆
松 松 松

zhǐ   *finger; to point*

指 指 指 指 指 指

shòu   *to give*

授 授 授 授 授 授

tǎo   *to demand; to ask (for something) back*

討 讨 討 討 討
讨 讨 讨

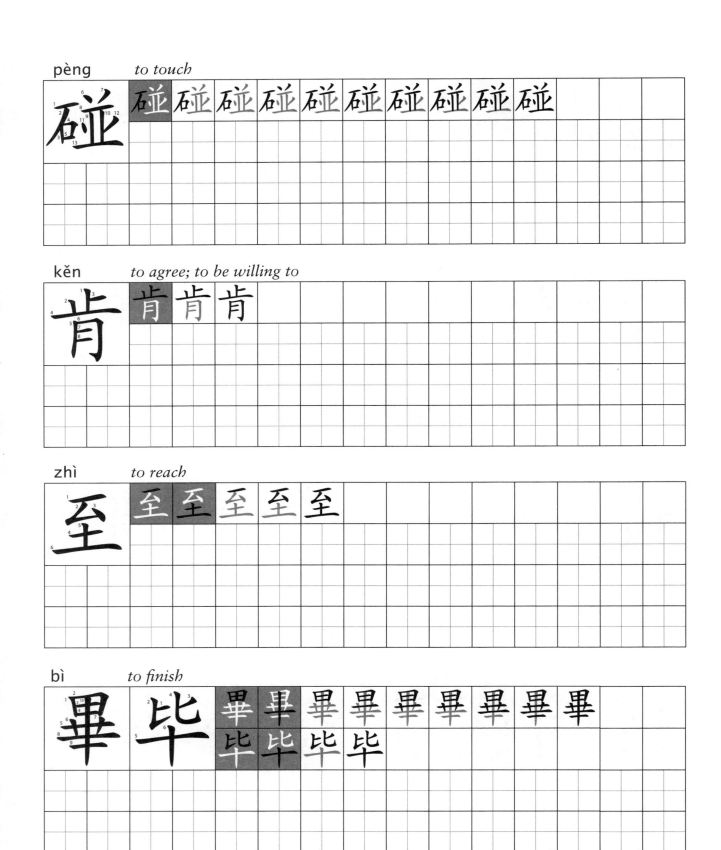

pèng   *to touch*

碰 碰 碰 碰 碰 碰 碰 碰 碰 碰 碰

kěn   *to agree; to be willing to*

肯 肯 肯 肯

zhì   *to reach*

至 至 至 至 至 至

bì   *to finish*

畢 毕 畢 畢 畢 畢 畢 畢 畢 畢
       毕 毕 毕 毕

jì   *to provide relief; to help*

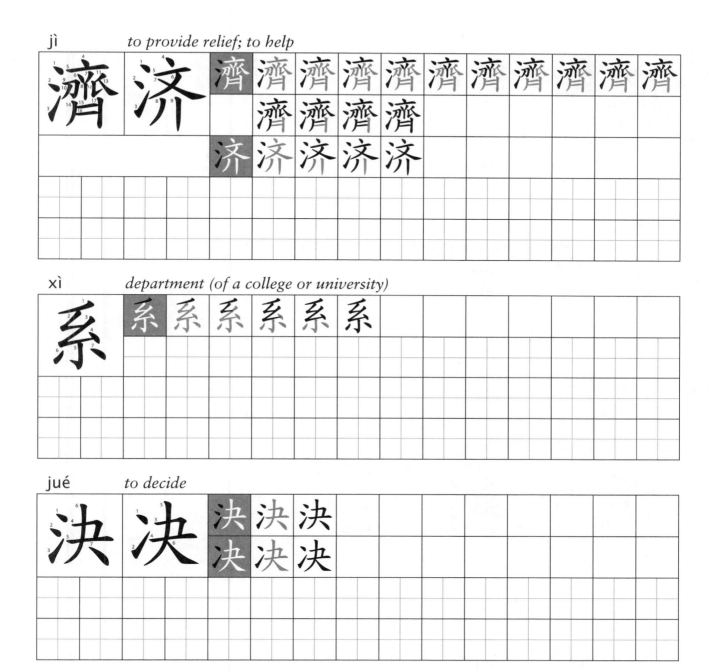

xì   *department (of a college or university)*

jué   *to decide*

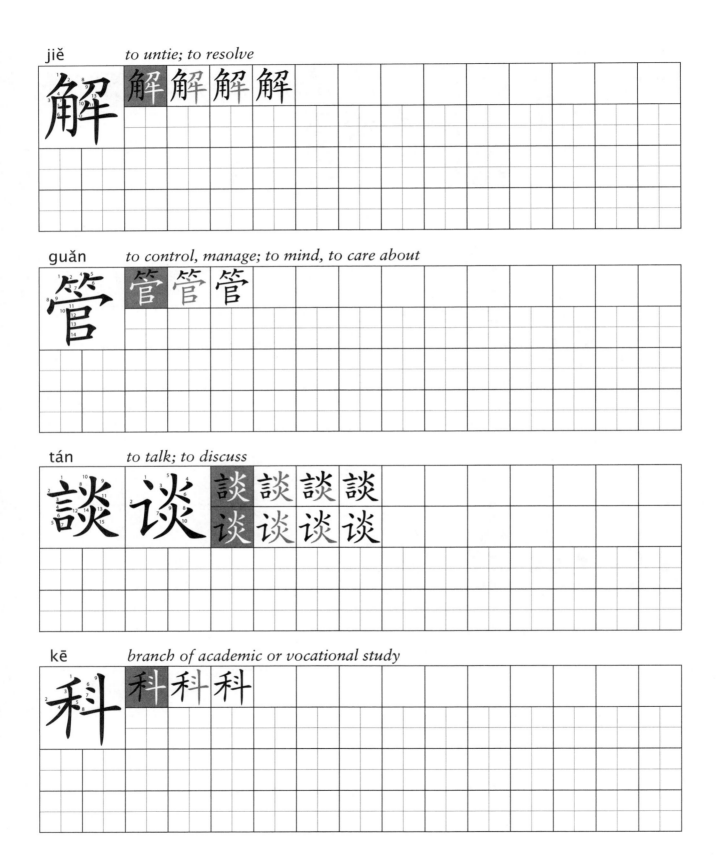

jiě   *to untie; to resolve*

guǎn   *to control, manage; to mind, to care about*

tán   *to talk; to discuss*

kē   *branch of academic or vocational study*

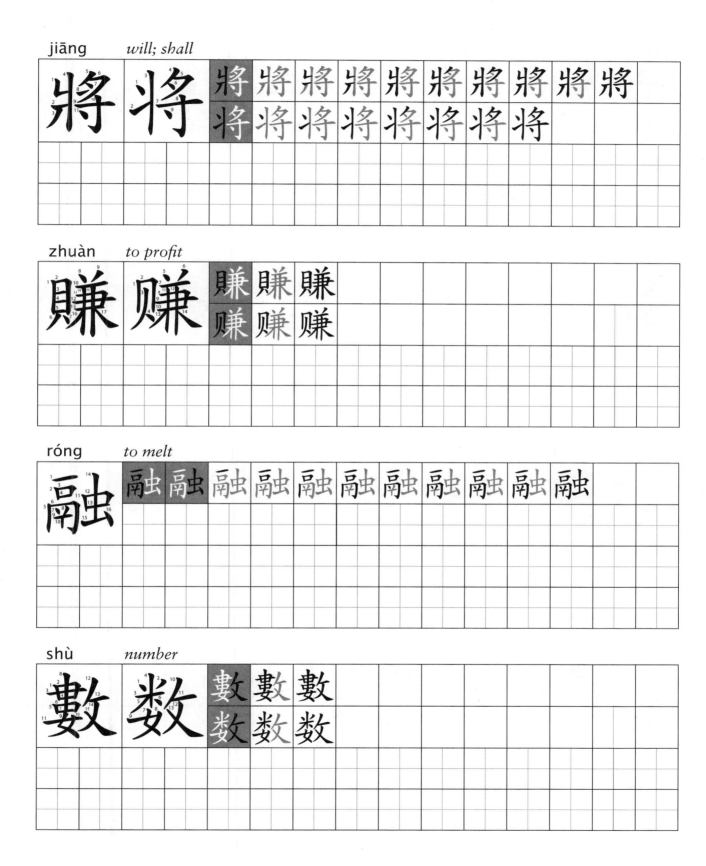

jiāng   *will; shall*

將 將 將 將 將 將 將 將 將 將 將

將 將 將 將 將 將 將 將

zhuàn   *to profit*

賺 賺 賺 賺

賺 賺 賺

róng   *to melt*

融 融 融 融 融 融 融 融 融 融 融

shù   *number*

數 數 數 數

數 数 数

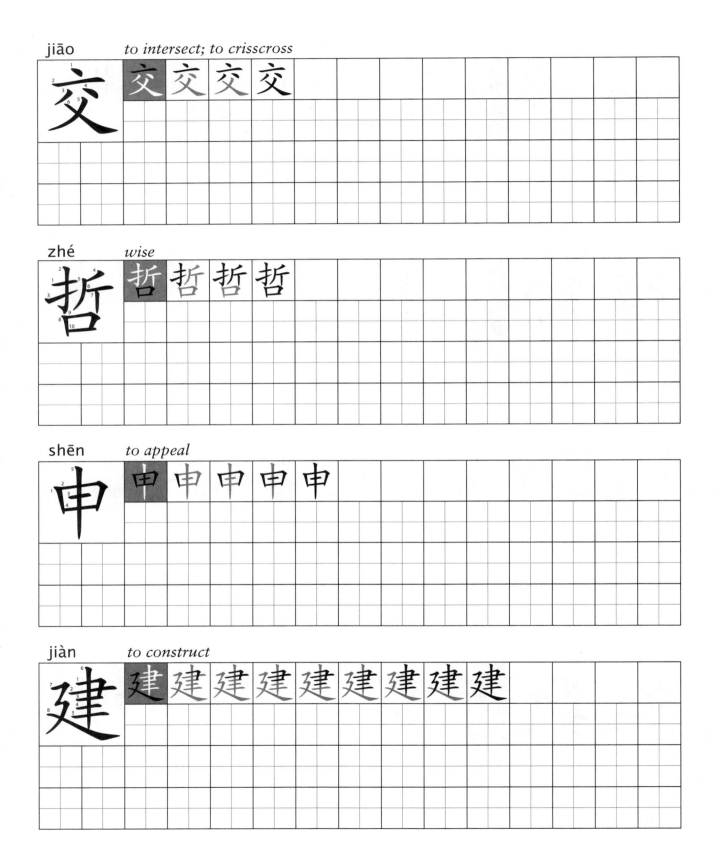

jiāo   *to intersect; to crisscross*

交

zhé   *wise*

哲

shēn   *to appeal*

申

jiàn   *to construct*

建

yì   *to discuss; to deliberate*

議 议 議 議 議 議

yàn   *to test*

驗 验 驗 驗 驗

Chinese Character Crosswords

Fill out the puzzles based on the *pinyin* clues provided. The common character is positioned in the center of the cluster of rings. The arrows indicate which way you should read the words.

1.

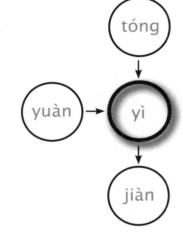

2.

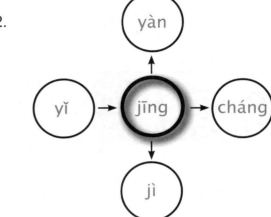

3.

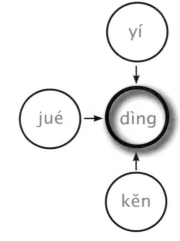

Integrated Chinese

nào   *noisy*

biè   *intractable*

niǔ, niu   *to twist*

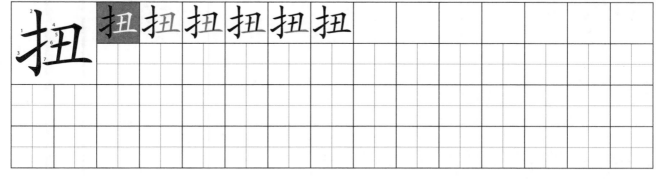

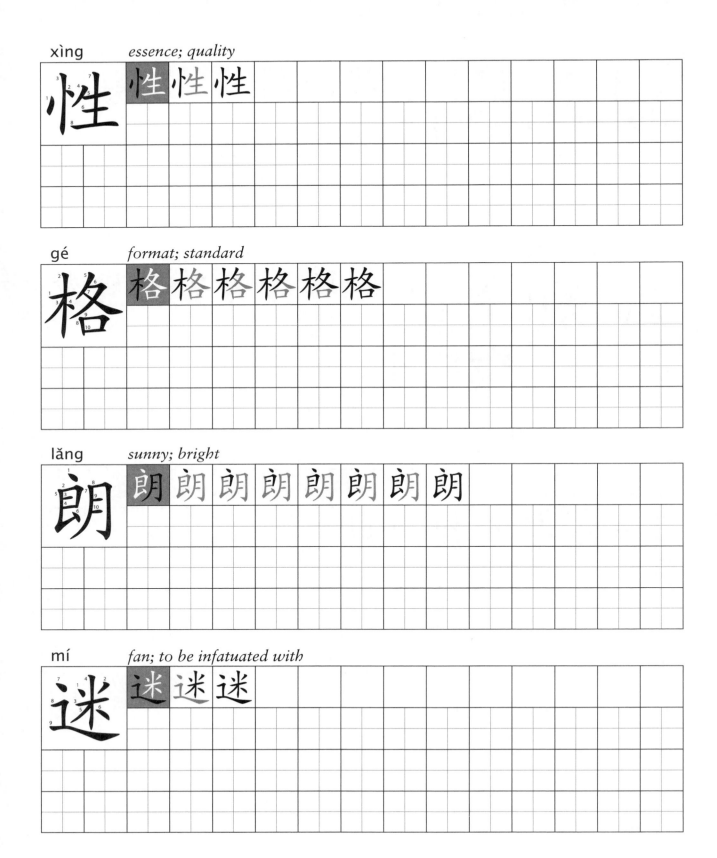

xìng   *essence; quality*

性   性 性 性

gé   *format; standard*

格   格 格 格 格 格 格

lǎng   *sunny; bright*

朗   朗 朗 朗 朗 朗 朗 朗

mí   *fan; to be infatuated with*

迷   迷 迷 迷

xiāng   *mutual*

相　相 相 相 相

zhī   *(Classical Chinese, possessive pronoun)*

之　之 之 之

dǐ   *bottom*

底　底 底 底 底 底 底

bèi   *back*

背　背 背 背

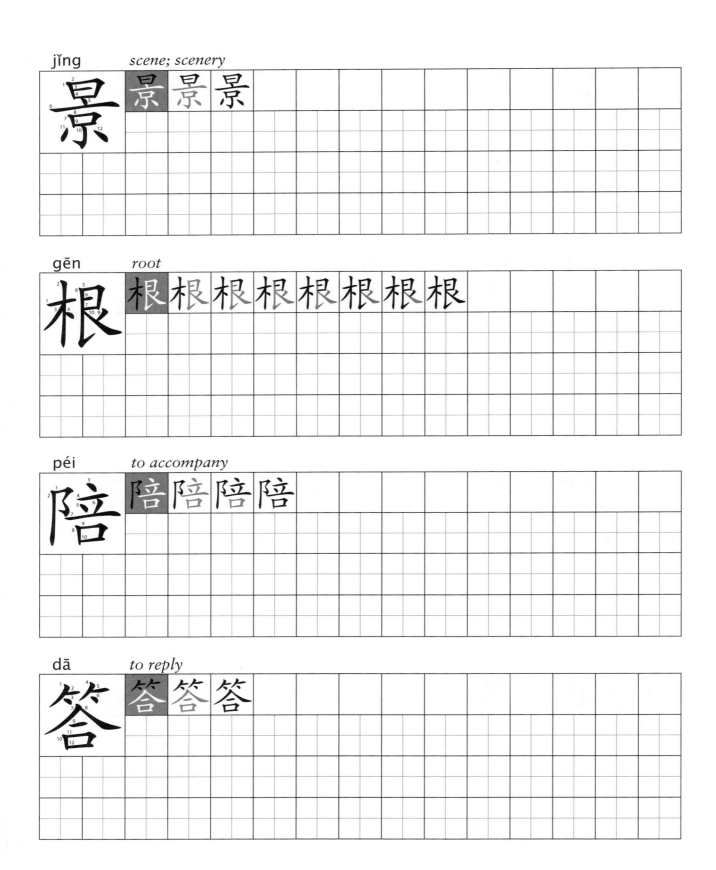

jǐng   *scene; scenery*
景

gēn   *root*
根

péi   *to accompany*
陪

dā   *to reply*
答

chuī   *to blow*

吹 吹 吹 吹 吹 吹

ō   *oh*

噢 噢 噢 噢 噢 噢 噢 噢 噢 噢
噢 噢 噢 噢 噢 噢 噢

yuán   *original*

原 原 原 原 原

hǔ   *tiger*

虎 虎 虎 虎

guài   *strange; to blame*

怪　怪 怪 怪 怪

qíng   *feeling; emotion*

情　情 情 情

tíng   *to stop*

停　停 停 停 停 停 停

qiàn   *regret*

歉　歉 歉 歉

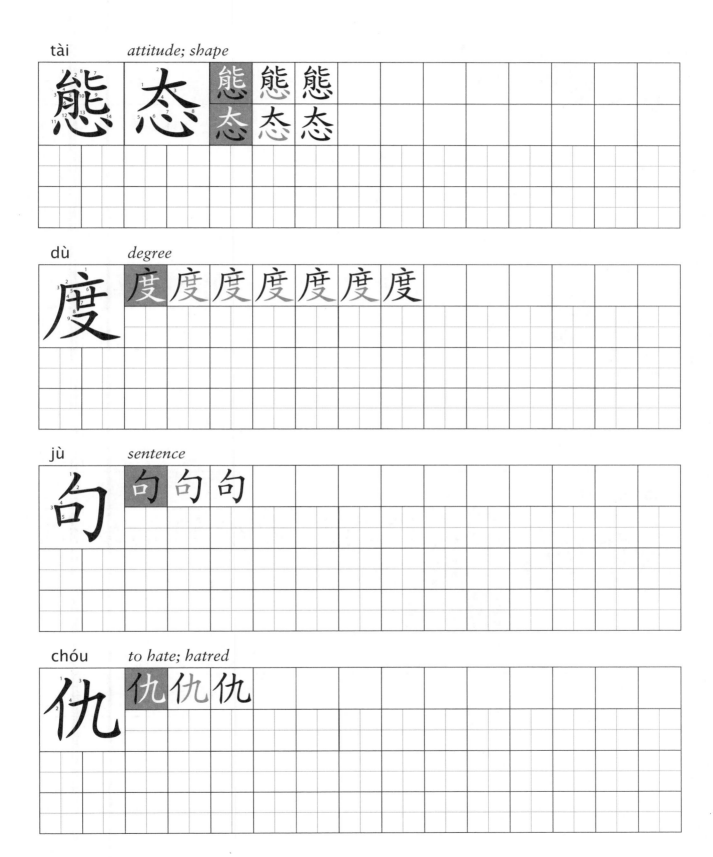

tài   *attitude; shape*

態   态   態 態 態
          态 态 态

dù   *degree*

度   度 度 度 度 度 度

jù   *sentence*

句   句 句 句

chóu   *to hate; hatred*

仇   仇 仇 仇

hā   *(imitating laughter)*

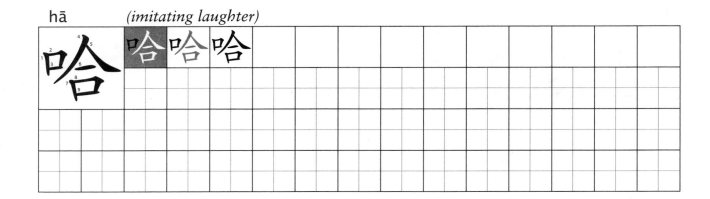

diū   *to lose*

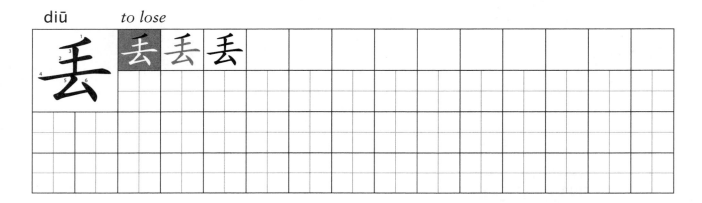

yào   *key*

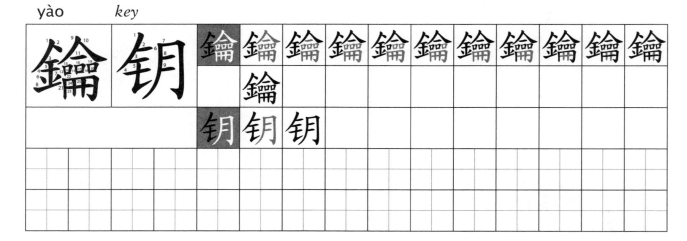

shi   *key*

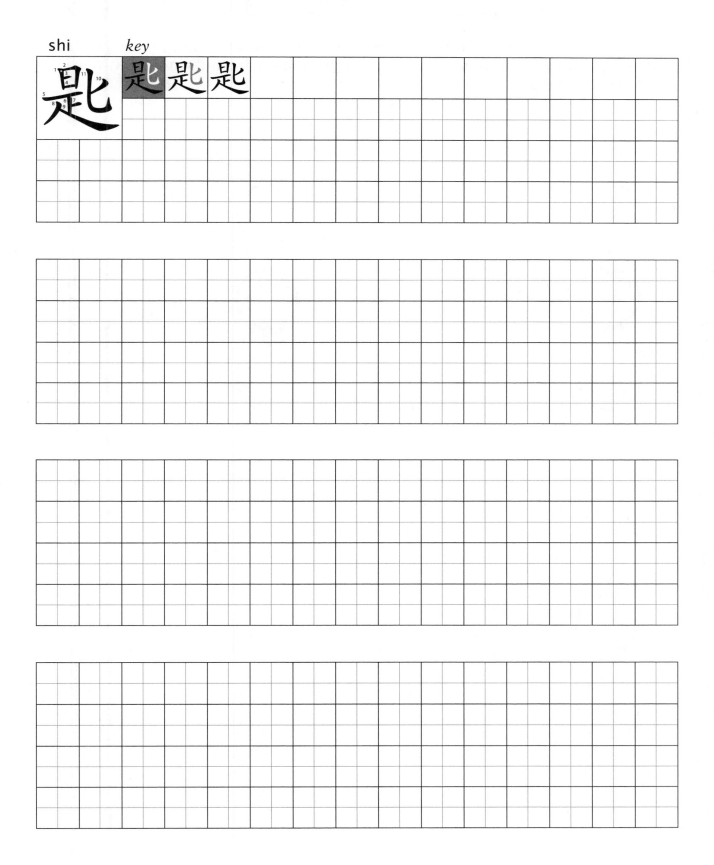

Chinese Character Crosswords

Fill out the puzzles based on the *pinyin* clues provided. The common character is positioned in the center of the cluster of rings. The arrows indicate which way you should read the words.

1.
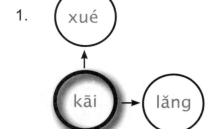

2.
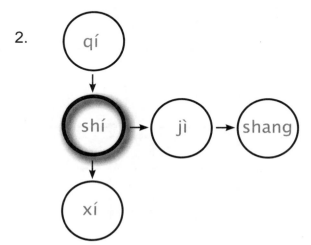

3
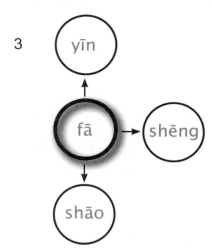

Integrated Chinese

luò   *net; nexus*

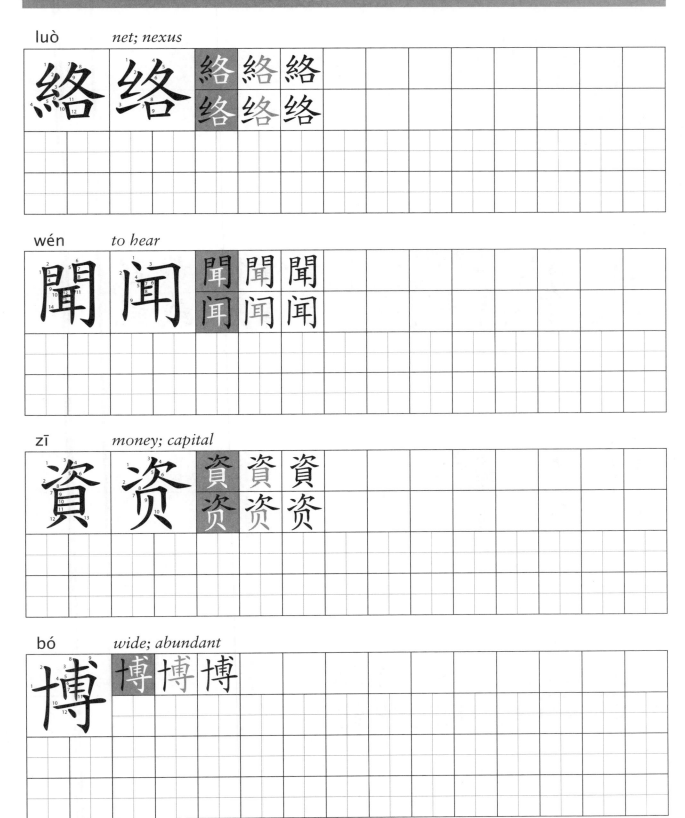

wén   *to hear*

zī   *money; capital*

bó   *wide; abundant*

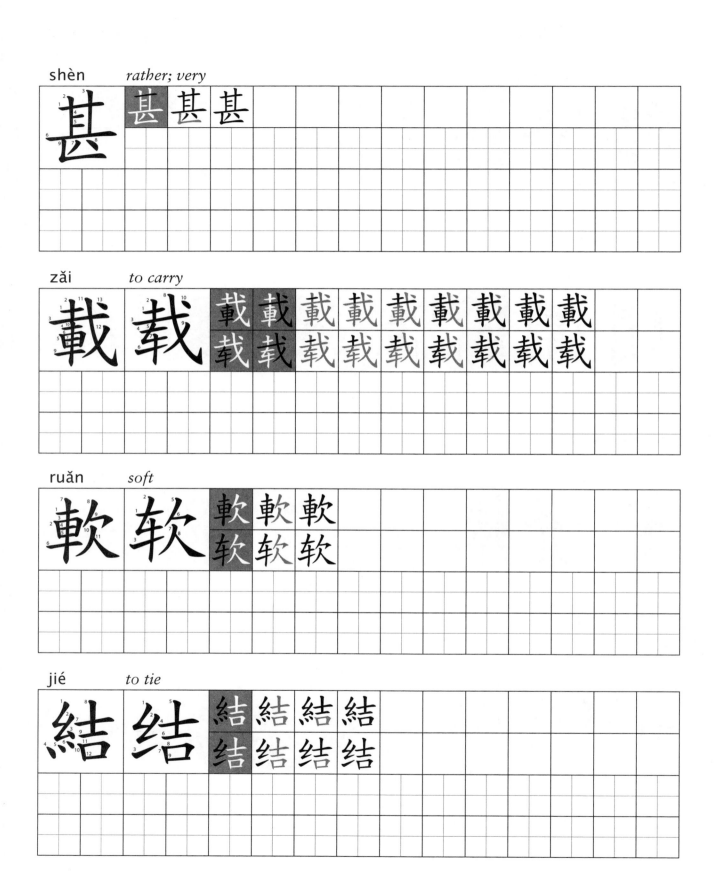

shèn   *rather; very*

zăi   *to carry*

ruăn   *soft*

jié   *to tie*

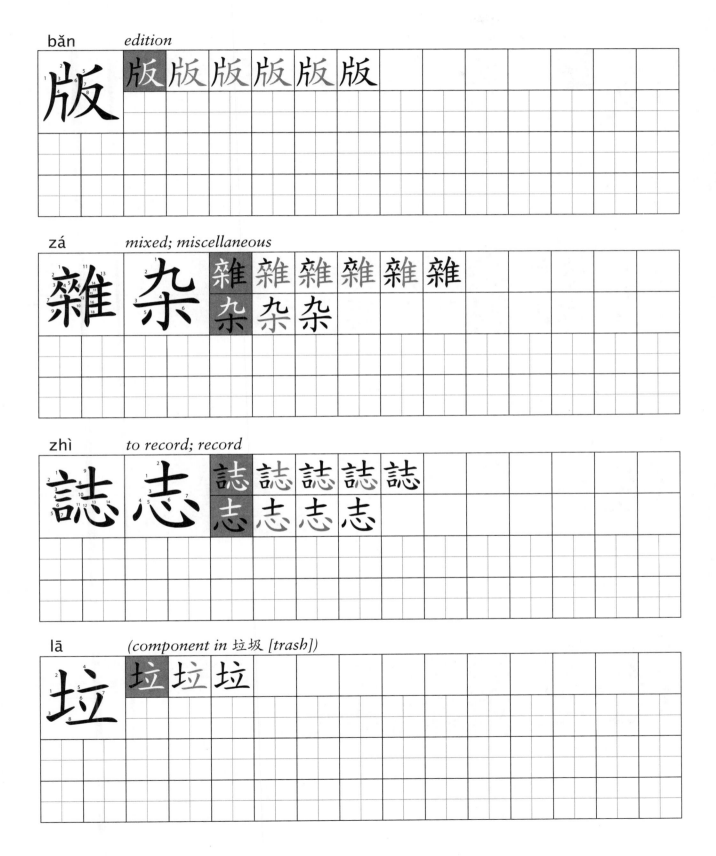

bǎn   *edition*

版

版 版 版 版 版 版

zá   *mixed; miscellaneous*

雜 杂

雜 雜 雜 雜 雜 雜
杂 杂 杂

zhì   *to record; record*

誌 志

誌 誌 誌 誌 誌
志 志 志 志

lā   *(component in 垃圾 [trash])*

垃

垃 垃 垃

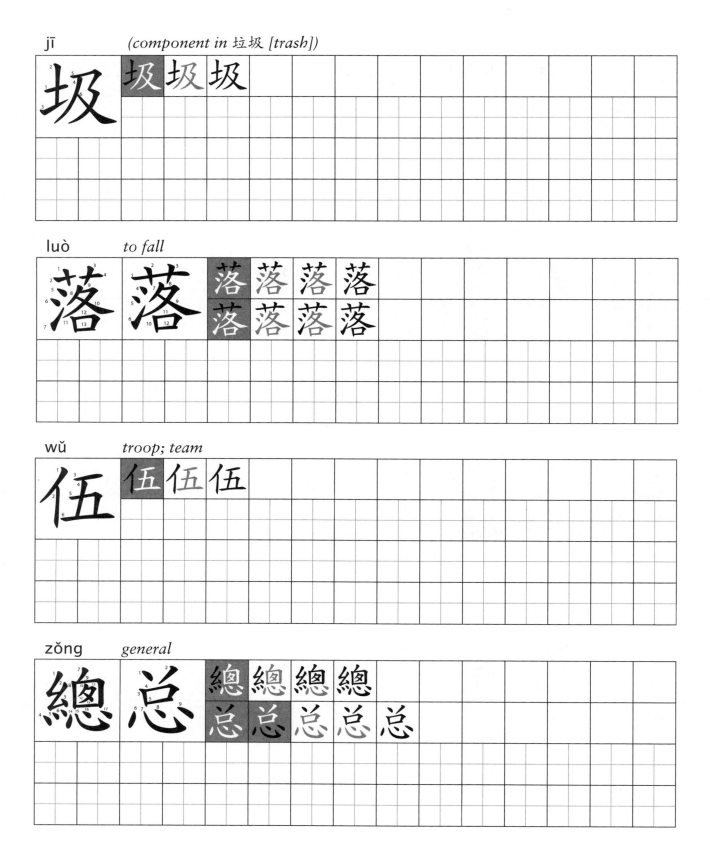

jī   (component in 垃圾 [trash])

坂

luò   to fall

落 落

wǔ   troop; team

伍

zǒng   general

總 总

chí   *late*

遲   迟   遲 遲 遲 遲 遲
            迟 迟 迟 迟

hài   *to cause trouble; to do harm to*

害   害 害 害 害 害 害 害

gǎn   *to dare*

敢   敢 敢 敢 敢

dāi   *to stay*

待   待 待 待

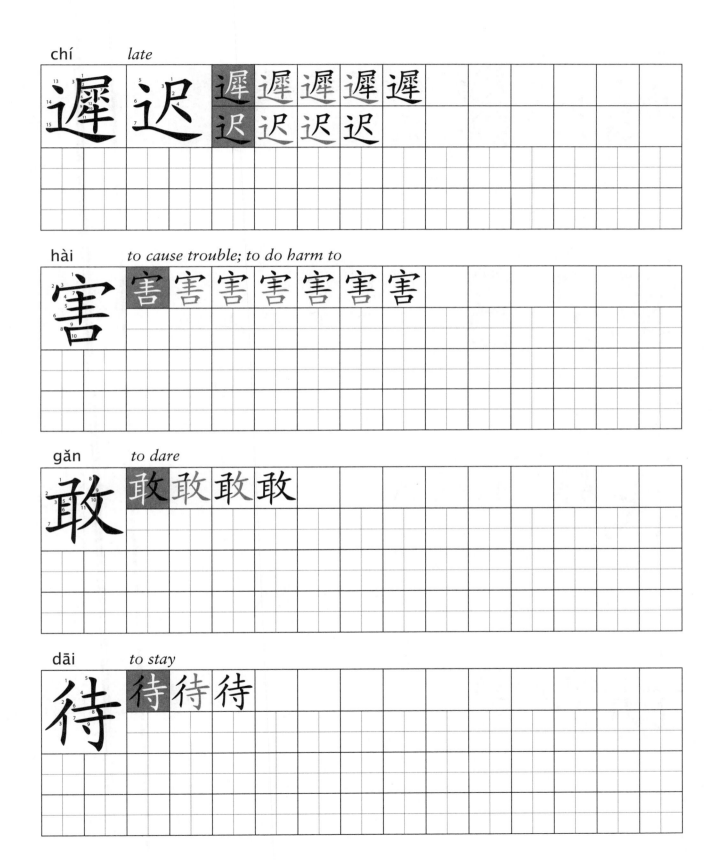

yǐn   *addiction*

瘾 瘾 瘾 瘾 瘾 瘾 瘾 瘾 瘾

yán   *serious; strict*

严 严 严 严 严 严 严 严 严 严

dài   *era; generation*

代 代 代 代 代 代

zhù   *to assist*

助 助 助 助

fān   *to turn over*

翻　翻 翻 翻 翻 翻 翻 翻 翻

yì   *to translate*

譯 译　譯 譯 譯 譯 譯 譯 譯
译 译 译 译 译 译

miǎn   *to exempt*

免　免 免 免 免 免 免

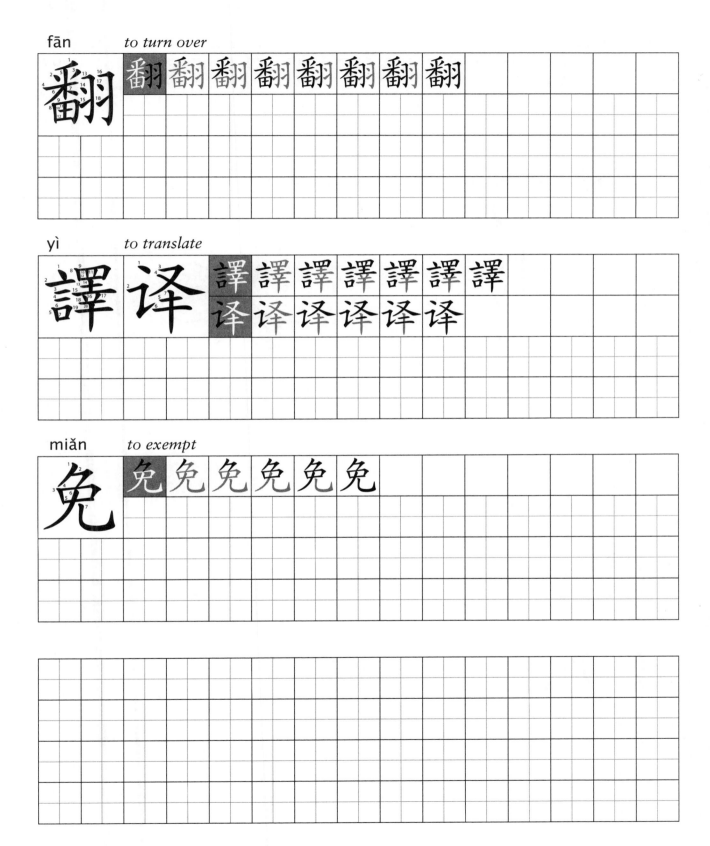

Chinese Character Crosswords

Fill out the puzzles based on the *pinyin* clues provided. The common character is positioned in the center of the cluster of rings. The arrows indicate which way you should read the words.

1.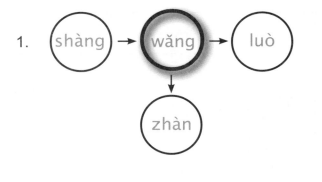

2.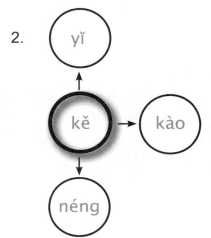

3.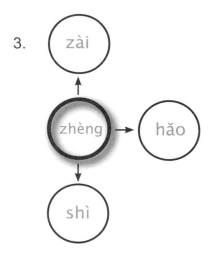

Integrated Chinese

rù — *to enter*

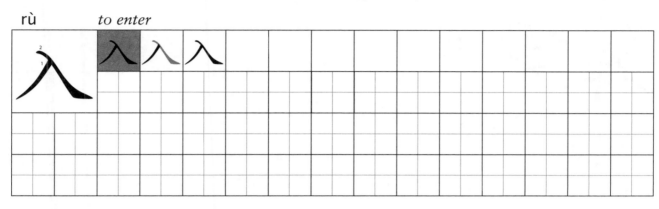

gōng — *to provide; to support financially*

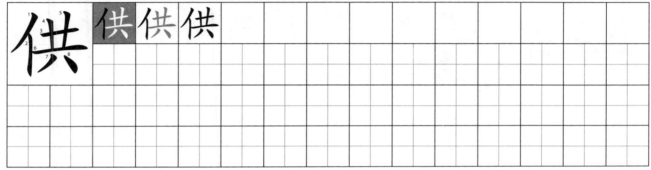

liáng — *good; excellent*

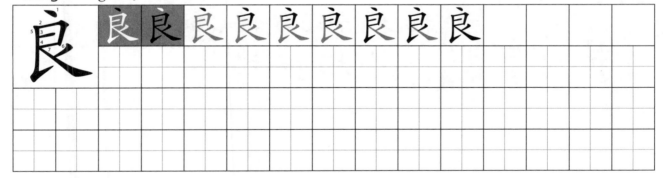

yù — *to cultivate; to educate*

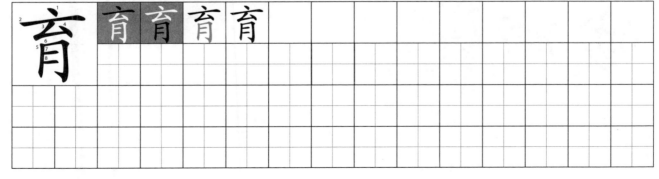

cún   *to save up; to deposit*

存

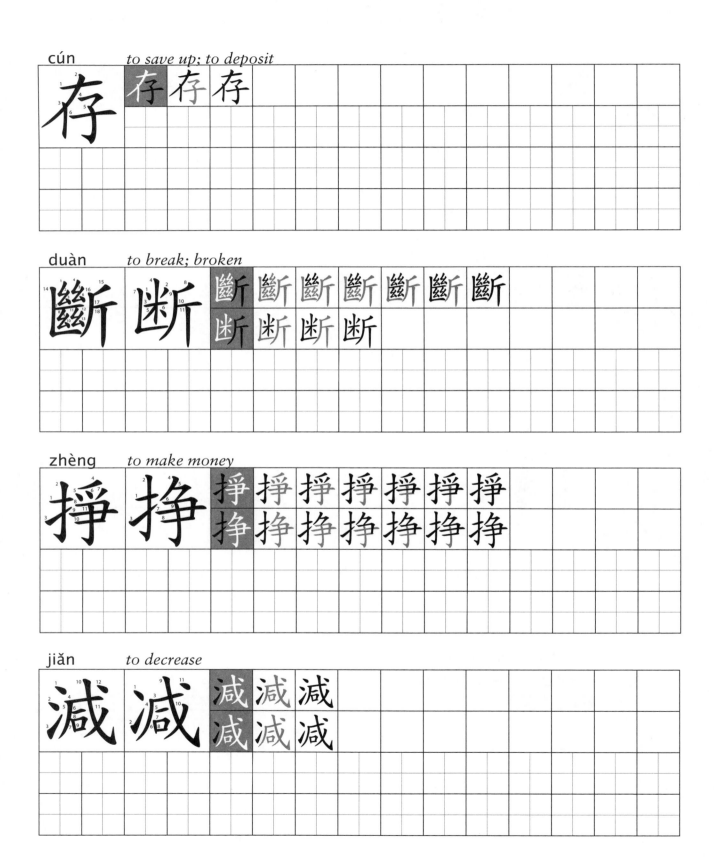

duàn   *to break; broken*

zhèng   *to make money*

jiǎn   *to decrease*

fù   *to shoulder; to bear burden*

負　负　負負負負
　　　負負负负

xiǎng   *loud*

響　响　響響響響響響響響
　　　响响响响响响

tíng   *courtyard*

庭　庭庭庭庭庭庭庭

qǔ   *to obtain*

取　取取取取

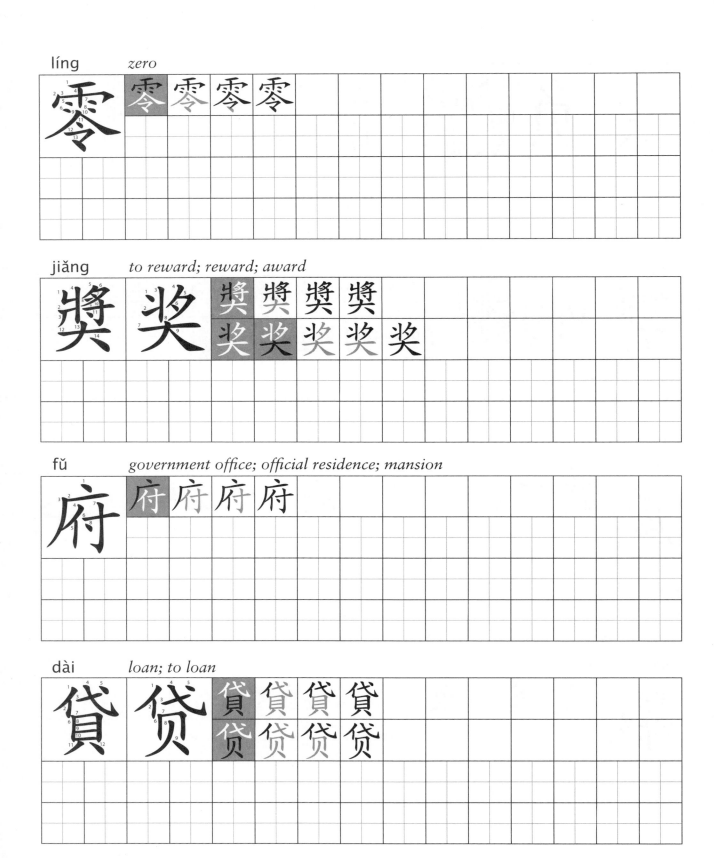

líng   *zero*

零

jiǎng   *to reward; reward; award*

獎 奖

fǔ   *government office; official residence; mansion*

府

dài   *loan; to loan*

貸 贷

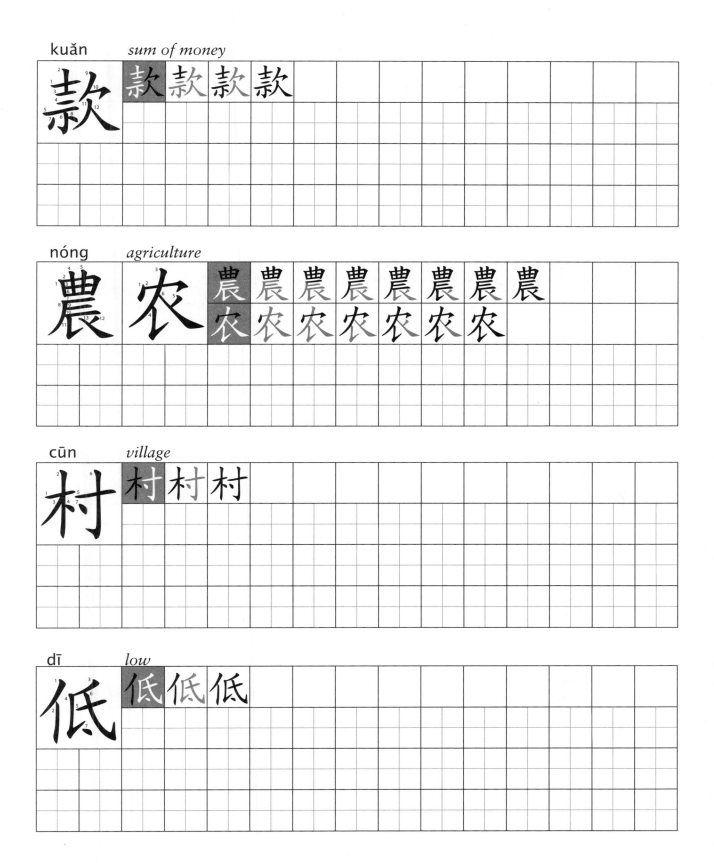

kuǎn　*sum of money*

款　款　款　款

nóng　*agriculture*

農　农　農　農　農　農　農　農　農
　　　农　农　农　农　农　农　农

cūn　*village*

村　村　村　村

dī　*low*

低　低　低　低

dú   *to read; to study*

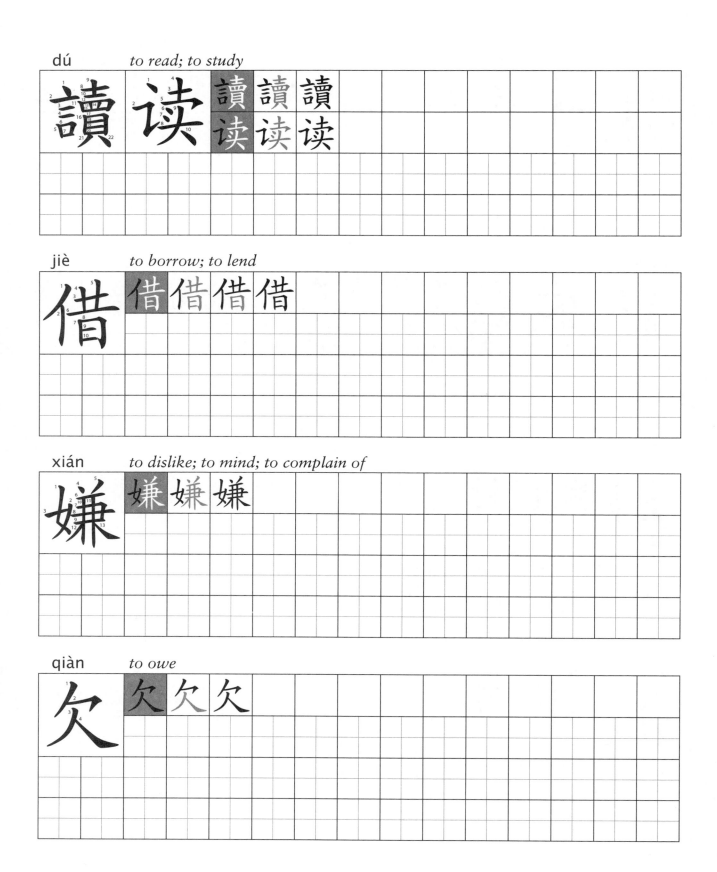

jiè   *to borrow; to lend*

xián   *to dislike; to mind; to complain of*

qiàn   *to owe*

yín   *silver*

銀 银 銀 銀 銀
        银 银 银

guāi   *(of children) obedient; well-behaved*

乖 乖 乖 乖 乖

Chinese Character Crosswords

Fill out the puzzles based on the *pinyin* clues provided. The common character is positioned in the center of the cluster of rings. The arrows indicate which way you should read the words.

1.

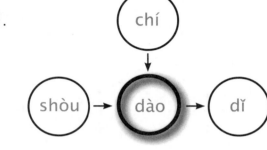

chí → dào

shòu → dào → dǐ

2.

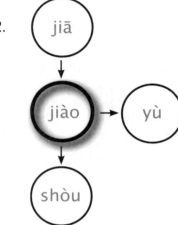

jiā → jiào

jiào → yù

jiào → shòu

3.

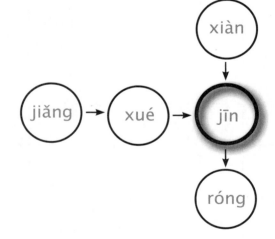

xiàn → jīn

jiǎng → xué → jīn

jīn → róng

Integrated Chinese

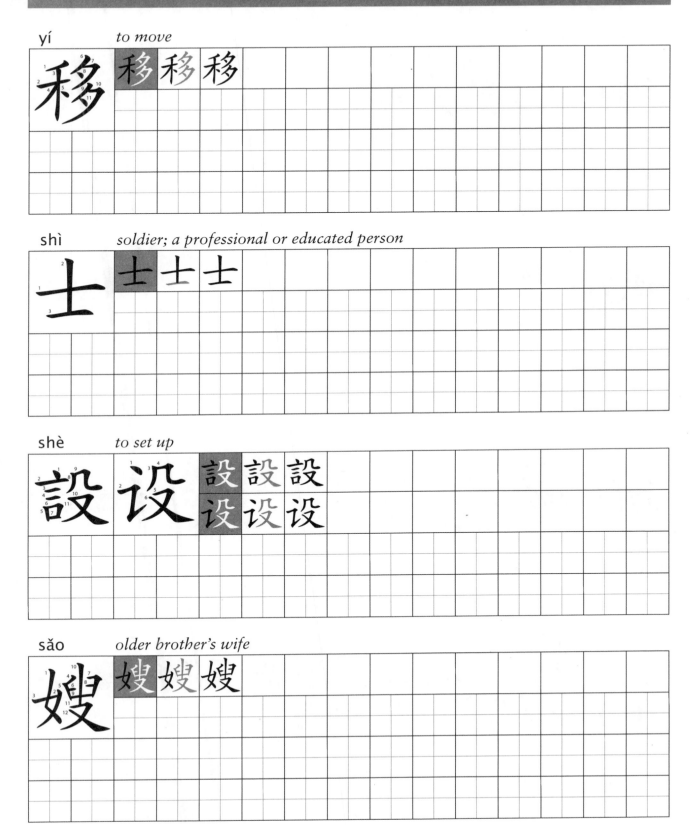

yí   *to move*

移 移 移 移

shì   *soldier; a professional or educated person*

士 士 士 士

shè   *to set up*

設 设 設 設 設 设 设 设

săo   *older brother's wife*

嫂 嫂 嫂 嫂

shuò   *ample; big*

硕 硕 硕 硕 硕
硕 硕 硕

hūn   *marriage; married*

婚 婚 婚 婚 婚

mǎn   *full*

满 满 满 满 满
满 满 满 满

lì   *severe*

厲 厲 厲 厲 厲 厲 厲 厲 厲
厉 厉 厉 厉 厉

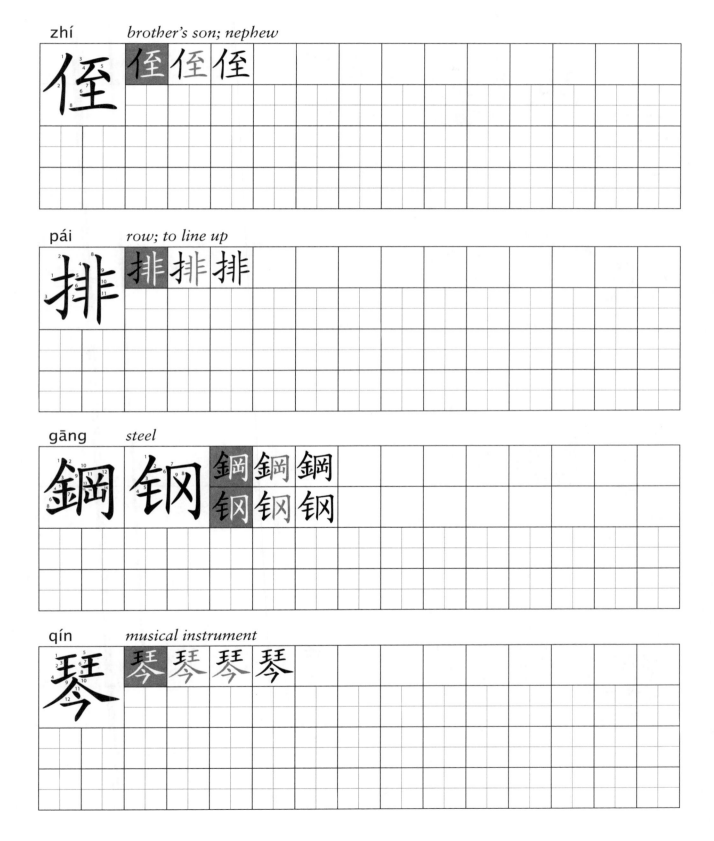

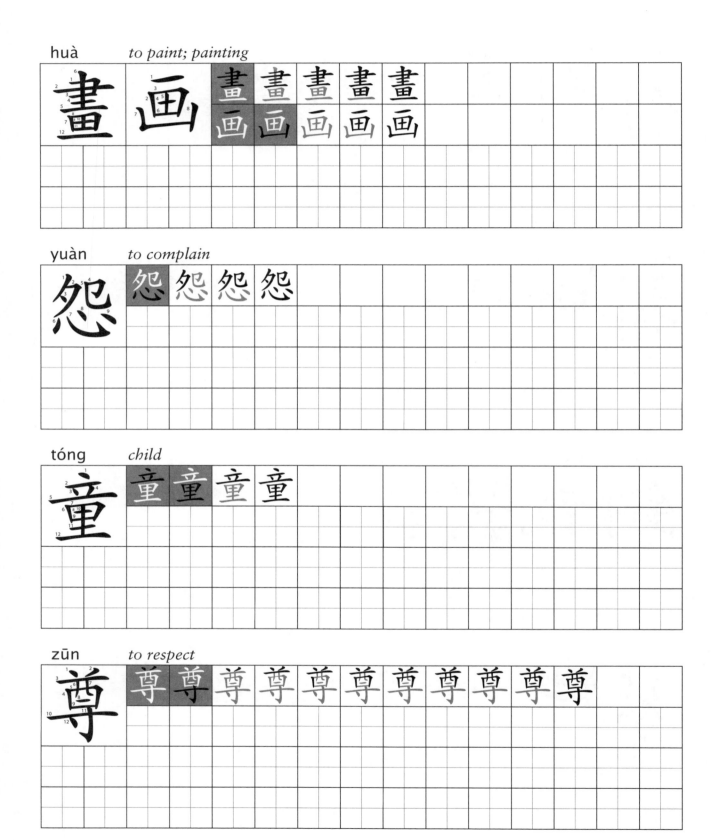

huà   *to paint; painting*

畫   画   畫   畫   畫   畫   畫
           画   画   画   画   画

yuàn   *to complain*

怨   怨   怨   怨   怨

tóng   *child*

童   童   童   童   童

zūn   *to respect*

尊   尊   尊   尊   尊   尊   尊   尊   尊   尊

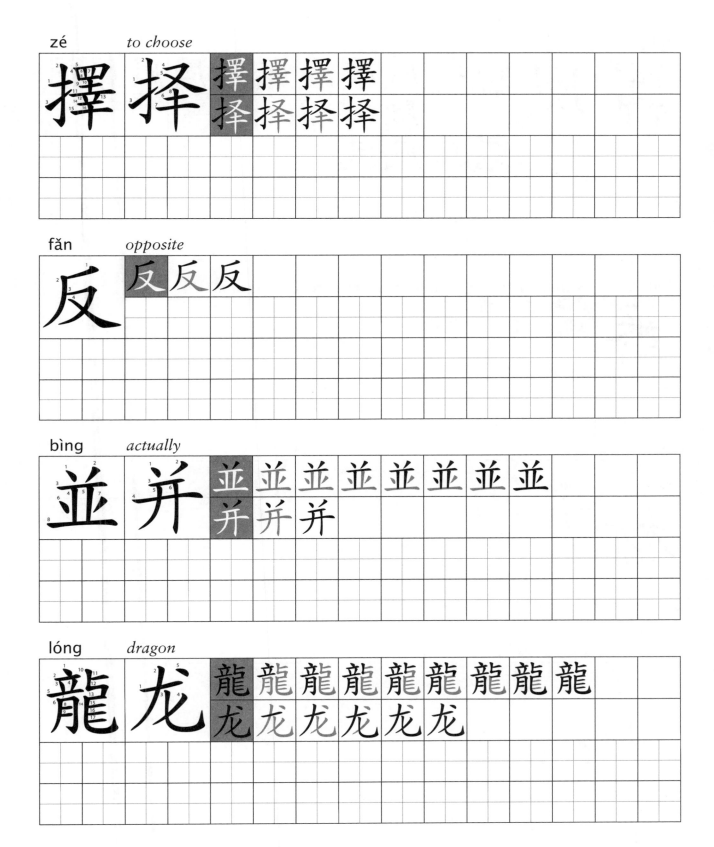

zé　*to choose*

擇　择

fǎn　*opposite*

反

bìng　*actually*

並　并

lóng　*dragon*

龍　龙

fèng   *phoenix*

鳳   凤

fān   *(measure word for rounds; measure word for type or kind)*

番

cái   *material*

材

Character from Proper Nouns

mò *ink*

墨 墨 墨 墨 墨

Chinese Character Crosswords

Fill out the puzzles based on the *pinyin* clues provided. The common character is positioned in the center of the cluster of rings. The arrows indicate which way you should read the words.

1.

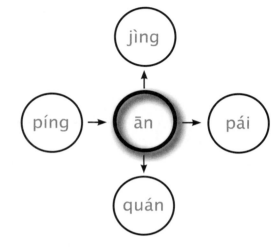

2.

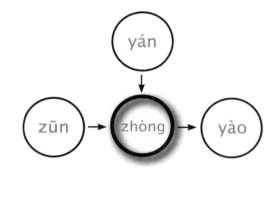

3.

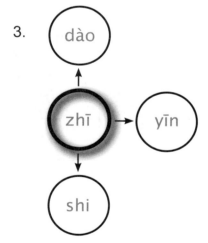

4.

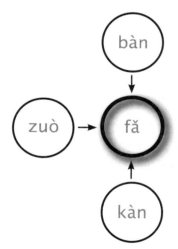

Integrated Chinese

Lesson 10

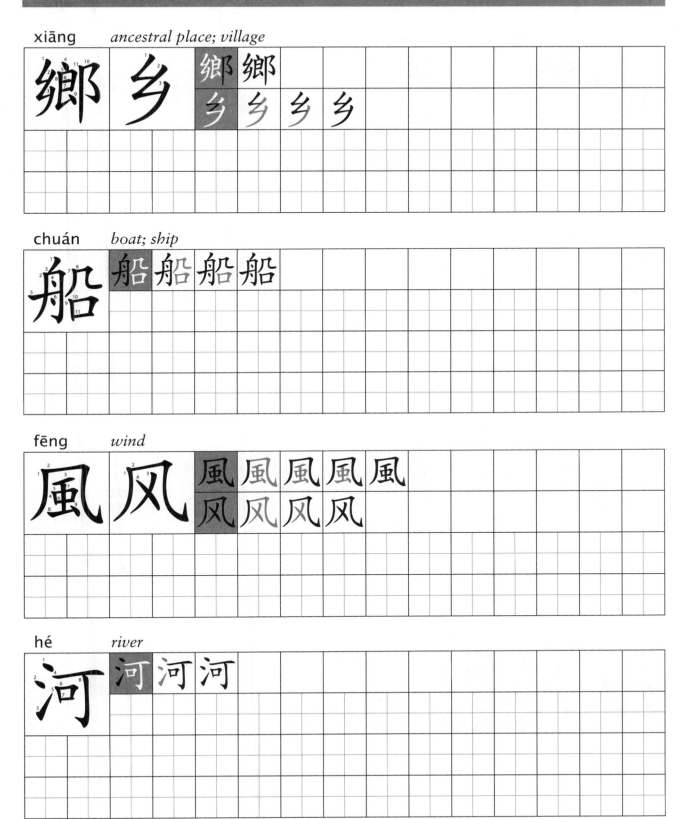

xiāng   *ancestral place; village*

鄉   乡

chuán   *boat; ship*

船

fēng   *wind*

風   风

hé   *river*

河

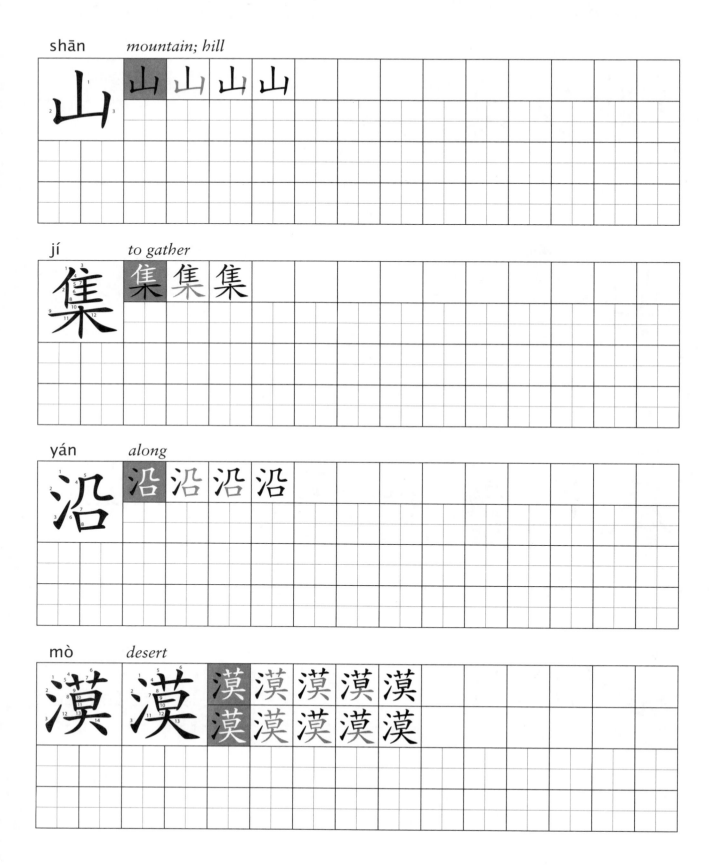

shān   *mountain; hill*

山   山 山 山 山

jí   *to gather*

集   集 集 集

yán   *along*

沿   沿 沿 沿 沿

mò   *desert*

漠 漠   漠 漠 漠 漠 漠
漠 漠 漠 漠 漠

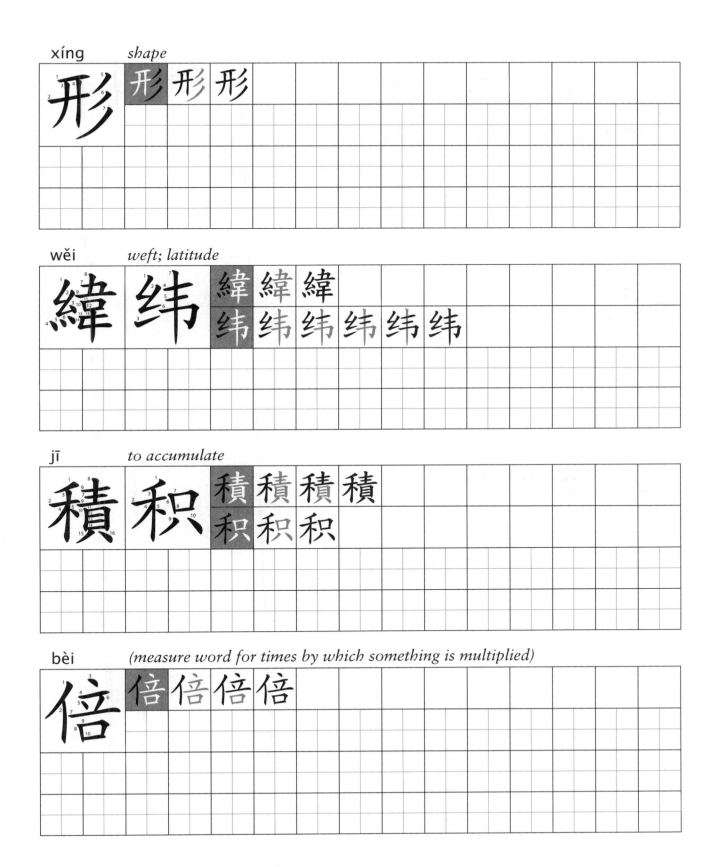

xíng   *shape*

形

wěi   *weft; latitude*

緯 纬

jī   *to accumulate*

積 积

bèi   *(measure word for times by which something is multiplied)*

倍

jǐ   *crowded; to push against; to squeeze*

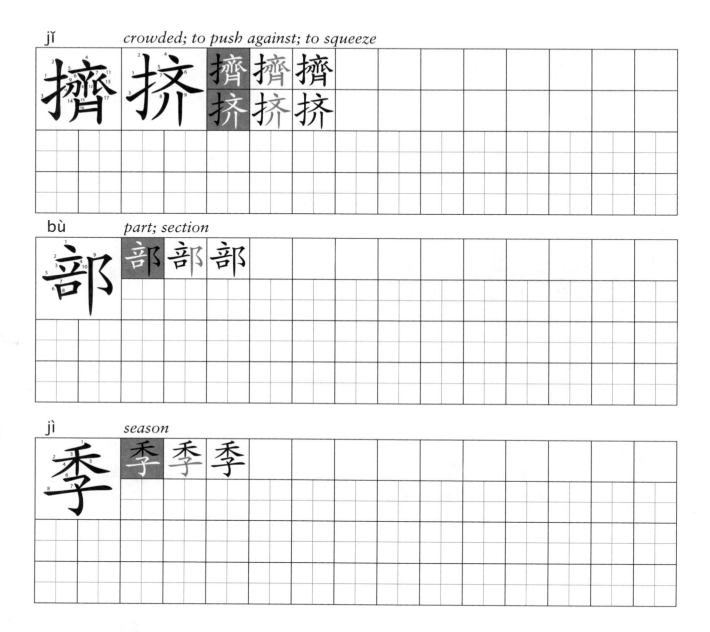

bù   *part; section*

jì   *season*

Characters from Proper Nouns

zú   *ethnic or social group*

族

ěr   *(Classical Chinese, second person pronoun)*

bīn   *shore*

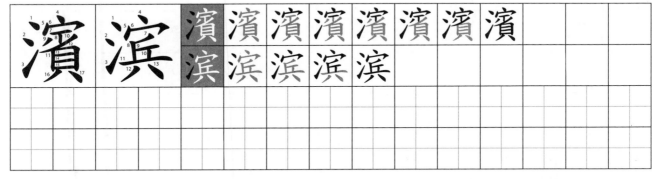

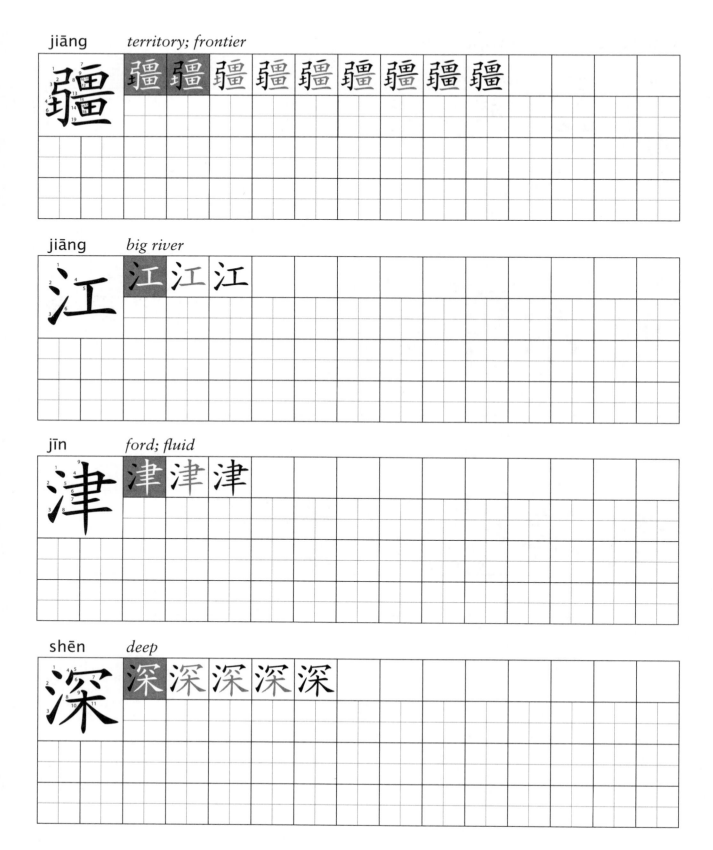

jiāng   *territory; frontier*

疆 疆 疆 疆 疆 疆 疆 疆 疆 疆

jiāng   *big river*

江 江 江 江

jīn   *ford; fluid*

津 津 津 津

shēn   *deep*

深 深 深 深 深 深

zhèn *ditch in a field*

圳 圳 圳 圳

yún *cloud*

雲 云 雲 雲 雲 雲
   云 云 云

Chinese Character Crosswords

Fill out the puzzles based on the *pinyin* clues provided. The common character is positioned in the center of the cluster of rings. The arrows indicate which way you should read the words.

1.

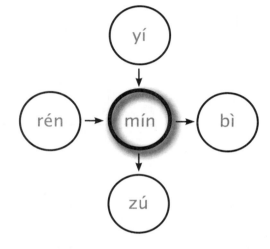

2.

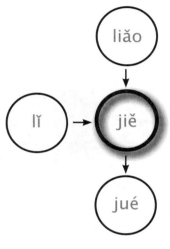

3.

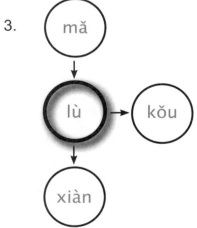

4.

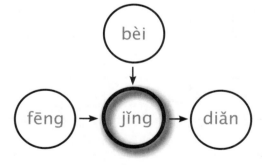

Chinese Character Crosswords

5.

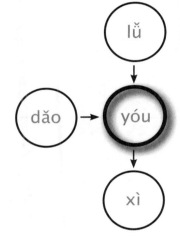

6.

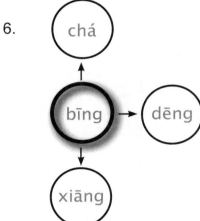

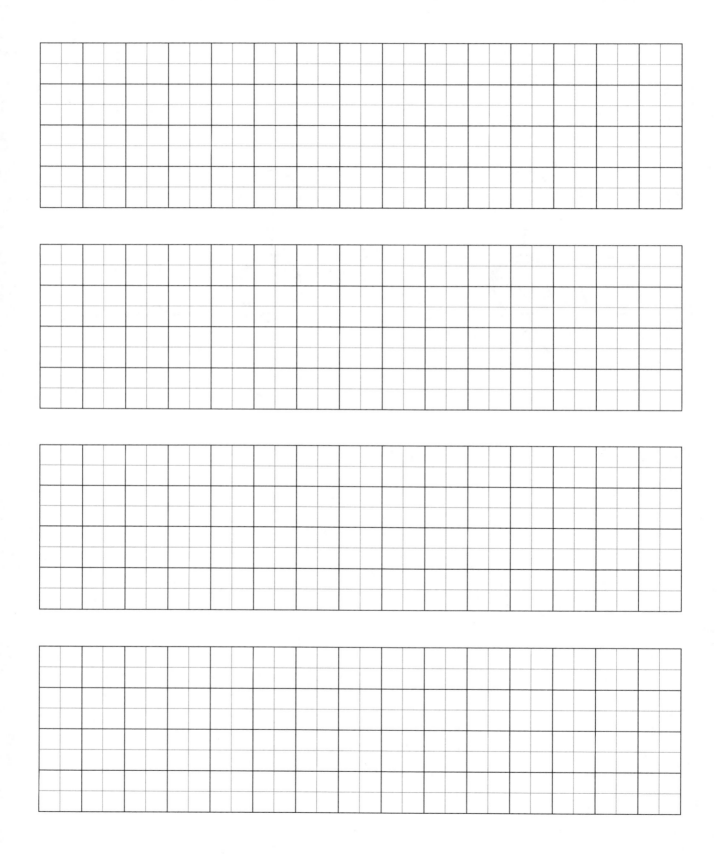

INDEX A
Characters by Pinyin

P = pinyin
T = traditional form
S = simplified form
L = lesson

guài	怪		strange; to blame	6	42
guǎn	管		to control, manage; to mind, to care about	5	32
guì	櫃	柜	cupboard; cabinet	2	5
hā	哈		(imitating laughter)	6	44
hài	害		to cause trouble; to do harm to	7	51
hé	河		river	10	71
hóng	烘		to bake	2	7
hū,hu	乎		(Classical Chinese) in; at	4	23
hú	湖		lake	3	16
hǔ	虎		tiger	6	41
huà	畫	画	to paint; painting	9	66
hūn	婚		marriage; married	9	64
jī	雞	鸡	chicken	3	11
jī	圾		(component in 垃圾 [trash])	7	50
jī	積	积	to accumulate	10	73
jí	急		urgent	2	8
jí	集		to gather	10	72
jǐ	擠		crowded; to push against; to squeeze	10	74
jì	濟	济	to provide relief; to help	5	31
jì	季		season	10	74
jià	價	价	price	4	21
jiǎn	減	减	to decrease	8	56
jiàn	建		to construct	5	34
jiāng	將	将	will; shall	5	33
jiāng	疆		territory; frontier	10	76
jiāng	江		big river	10	76
jiǎng	獎	奖	to reward; reward; award	8	58
jiāo	交		to intersect; to crisscross	5	34
jiào	較	较	to compare	1	2
jié	結	结	to tie	7	48
jiě	解		to untie; to resolve	5	32
jiè	芥	芥	mustard greens	3	11
jiè	界		realm	5	27
jiè	借		to borrow; to lend	8	60
jīn	巾		towel; scarf	3	14
jīn	津		ford; fluid	10	76
jǐng	景		scene; scenery	6	40
jiū	究		to investigate	1	1
jiù	舊	旧	(of things) old	2	6
jù	句		sentence	6	43
jué	決	决	to decide	5	31
kē	柯		(a surname); handle of an axe; stem	1	3
kē	科		branch of academic or vocational study	5	32
kěn	肯		to agree; to be willing to	5	30
kǒng	恐		to fear	2	7
kuǎn	款		sum of money	8	59
lā	垃		(component in 垃圾 [trash])	7	49
là	拉		to leave (something) behind	1	3
lán	蘭	兰	orchid	3	12
lǎng	朗		sunny; bright	6	38
lì	麗	丽	beautiful	3	15
lì	歷	历	to experience; experience	5	27
lì	厲	厉	severe	9	64
lián	廉		cheap; inexpensive	4	23
liáng	良		good; excellent	8	55
liàng	輛	辆	(measure word for vehicles)	1	1
liàng	量		quantity	4	22
líng	零		zero	8	58
liú	留		to leave behind	3	11
liú	流		to flow	3	14
lóng	龍	龙	dragon	9	67

lǜ	慮	虑	to worry; worry	3	14
lùn	論	论	theory; to discuss	4	19
luò	絡	络	net; nexus	7	47
luò	落	落	to fall	7	50
mǎn	滿	满	full	9	64
máo	髦		children's bangs	4	22
méi	梅		plum	3	15
mí	迷		fan; to be infatuated with	6	38
mián	棉		cotton	4	22
miǎn	免		to exempt	7	53
mò	墨		ink	9	69
mò	漠	漠	desert	10	72
nào	鬧	闹	noisy	6	37
nèi	內		inside; inner	1	1
nèn	嫩		tender	3	12
niǔ, niu	扭		to twist	6	37
nóng	農	农	agriculture	8	59
ō	噢	噢	oh	6	41
pái	排		row; to line up	9	65
péi	陪		to accompany	6	40
pèng	碰		to touch	5	30
pín	貧	贫	poor; annoyingly wordy or glib	4	24
pǐn	品		object; article	2	7
qí	其		(Classical Chinese, third person possessive pronoun)	5	28
qiàn	歉		regret	6	42
qiàn	欠		to owe	8	60
qín	琴		musical instrument	9	65
qíng	情		feeling; emotion	6	42
qīng	輕	轻	light	5	28
qǔ	取		to obtain	8	57
quán	全		complete	1	2
róng	融		to melt	5	33
rù	入		to enter	8	55
ruǎn	軟	软	soft	7	48

sǎo	嫂		older brother's wife	9	63
shā	莎	莎	sedge grass	3	15
shān	山		mountain; hill	10	72
shè	設	设	to set up	9	63
shēn	申		to appeal	5	34
shēn	深		deep	10	76
shèn	甚		rather; very	7	48
shěng	省		to save; to economize	1	2
shi	匙		key	6	45
shǐ	史		history	5	28
shì	世		world	5	27
shì	士		soldier; a professional or educated person	9	63
shòu	授		to give	5	29
shù	數	数	number	5	33
shuì	稅		tax	4	24
shuò	碩	硕	ample; big	9	64
sōng	鬆	松	loose; relaxed	5	29
tài	態	态	attitude; shape	6	43
tán	談	谈	to talk; to discuss	5	32
tǎn	毯		blanket	2	5
tǎo	討	讨	to demand; to ask (for something) back	5	29
tiáo	調	调	to regulate	2	6
tíng	停		to stop	6	42
tíng	庭		courtyard	8	57
tóng	童		child	9	66
wěi	緯	纬	weft; latitude	10	73
wén	聞	闻	to hear	7	47
wū	屋		room; house	2	5
wú	無	无	no; none	4	19
wǔ	伍		troop; team	7	50
xì	系		department (of a college or university)	5	31
xiān	鮮	鲜	fresh	3	12

xián	鹹	咸	salty	3	13
xián	嫌		to dislike; to mind; to complain of	8	60
xiāng	相		mutual	6	39
xiāng	鄉	乡	ancestral place; village	10	71
xiǎng	響	响	loud	8	57
xíng	形		shape	10	73
xìng	性		essence; quality	6	38
xū	需		to need	4	20
xù	恤		to pity	4	19
xuǎn	選	选	to choose	5	27
yá	牙		tooth	4	20
yán	研		to grind	1	1
yán	嚴	严	serious; strict	7	52
yán	沿		along	10	72
yàn	驗	验	to test	5	35
yào	鑰	钥	key	6	44
yí	移		to move	9	63
yì	議	议	to discuss; to deliberate	5	35
yì	譯	译	to translate	7	53
yín	銀	银	silver	8	61
yǐn	癮	瘾	addiction	7	52
yóu	由		from; out of	1	2
yóu	油		oil; oily	3	13
yú	於	于	(Classical Chinese) at; in	4	21
yù	育		to cultivate; to educate	8	55
yuán	原		original	6	41
yuàn	怨		to complain	9	66
yún	雲	云	cloud	10	77
zá	雜	杂	mixed; miscellaneous	7	49
zǎi	仔		boy; child	4	19
zǎi	載	载	to carry	7	48
zán	咱		we	4	24
zé	擇	择	to choose	9	67

zhāng	章		essay; article	5	28
zháo	着		to burn; to touch	2	8
zhé	哲		wise	5	34
zhèn	圳		ditch in a field	10	77
zhēng	蒸	蒸	to steam	3	11
zhèng	掙	挣	to make money	8	56
zhī	之		(Classical Chinese, possessive pronoun)	6	39
zhí	侄		brother's son; nephew	9	65
zhǐ	指		finger; to point	5	29
zhì	質	质	quality	4	22
zhì	至		to reach	5	30
zhì	誌	志	to record; record	7	49
zhǔ	主		main; chief	3	14
zhù	助		to assist	7	52
zhuàn	賺	赚	to profit	5	33
zī	資	资	money; capital	7	47
zǒng	總	总	general	7	50
zú	族		ethnic or social group	10	75
zūn	尊		to respect	9	66

INDEX B
(Characters by lesson and by pinyin)

P = pinyin
T = traditional form
S = simplified form
L = lesson

shuì	稅		tax	4	24
wú	無	无	no; none	4	19
xū	需		to need	4	20
xù	恤		to pity	4	19
yá	牙		tooth	4	20
yú	於	于	(Classical Chinese) at; in	4	21
zǎi	仔		boy; child	4	19
zán	咱		we	4	24
zhì	質	质	quality	4	22
bì	畢	毕	to finish	5	30
guǎn	管		to control, manage; to mind, to care about	5	32
jì	濟	济	to provide relief; to help	5	31
jiàn	建		to construct	5	34
jiāng	將	将	will; shall	5	33
jiāo	交		to intersect; to crisscross	5	34
jiě	解		to untie; to resolve	5	32
jiè	界		realm	5	27
jué	決	决	to decide	5	31
kē	科		branch of academic or vocational study	5	32
kěn	肯		to agree; to be willing to	5	30
lì	歷	历	to experience; experience	5	27
pèng	碰		to touch	5	30
qí	其		(Classical Chinese, third person possessive pronoun)	5	28
qīng	輕	轻	light	5	28
róng	融		to melt	5	33
shēn	申		to appeal	5	34
shǐ	史		history	5	28
shì	世		world	5	27
shòu	授		to give	5	29
shù	數	数	number	5	33
sōng	鬆	松	loose; relaxed	5	29
tán	談	谈	to talk; to discuss	5	32
tǎo	討	讨	to demand; to ask (for something) back	5	29
xì	系		department (of a college or university)	5	31
xuǎn	選	选	to choose	5	27
yàn	驗	验	to test	5	35
yì	議	议	to discuss; to deliberate	5	35
zhāng	章		essay; article	5	28
zhé	哲		wise	5	34
zhǐ	指		finger; to point	5	29
zhì	至		to reach	5	30
zhuàn	賺	赚	to profit	5	33
bèi	背		back	6	39
biè	彆	别	intractable	6	37
chóu	仇		to hate; hatred	6	43
chuī	吹		to blow	6	41
dā	答		to reply	6	40
dǐ	底		bottom	6	39
diū	丟		to lose	6	44
dù	度		degree	6	43
gé	格		format; standard	6	38
gēn	根		root	6	40
guài	怪		strange; to blame	6	42
hā	哈		(imitating laughter)	6	44
hǔ	虎		tiger	6	41
jǐng	景		scene; scenery	6	40
jù	句		sentence	6	43
lǎng	朗		sunny; bright	6	38
mí	迷		fan; to be infatuated with	6	38
nào	鬧	闹	noisy	6	37
niǔ, niu	扭		to twist	6	37
ō	噢	噢	oh	6	41
péi	陪		to accompany	6	40
qiàn	歉		regret	6	42

Pinyin	Traditional	Simplified	Meaning	Ch.	Pg.
fǎn	反		opposite	9	67
fèng	鳳	凤	phoenix	9	68
gāng	鋼	钢	steel	9	65
huà	畫	画	to paint; painting	9	66
hūn	婚		marriage; married	9	64
lì	屬	厉	severe	9	64
lóng	龍	龙	dragon	9	67
mǎn	滿	满	full	9	64
mò	墨		ink	9	69
pái	排		row; to line up	9	65
qín	琴		musical instrument	9	65
sǎo	嫂		older brother's wife	9	63
shè	設	设	to set up	9	63
shì	士		soldier; a professional or educated person	9	63
shuò	碩	硕	ample; big	9	64
tóng	童		child	9	66
yí	移		to move	9	63
yuàn	怨		to complain	9	66
zé	擇	择	to choose	9	67
zhí	侄		brother's son; nephew	9	65
zūn	尊		to respect	9	66
bèi	倍		(measure word for times by which something is multiplied)	10	73
bīn	濱	滨	shore	10	75
bù	部		part; section	10	74
chuán	船		boat; ship	10	71
ěr	爾	尔	(Classical Chinese, second person pronoun)	10	75
fēng	風	风	wind	10	71
hé	河		river	10	71
jī	積	积	to accumulate	10	73
jí	集		to gather	10	72
jǐ	擠		crowded; to push against; to squeeze	10	74
jì	季		season	10	74
jiāng	疆		territory; frontier	10	76
jiāng	江		big river	10	76
jīn	津		ford; fluid	10	76
mò	漠	漠	desert	10	72
shān	山		mountain; hill	10	72
shēn	深		deep	10	76
wěi	緯	纬	weft; latitude	10	73
xiāng	鄉	乡	ancestral place; village	10	71
xíng	形		shape	10	73
yán	沿		along	10	72
yún	雲	云	cloud	10	77
zhèn	圳		ditch in a field	10	77
zú	族		ethnic or social group	10	75